LEADING THE TEAM
AN ARCHITECT'S GUIDE TO DESIGN MANAGEMENT

DALE
SINCLAIR

RIBA Publishing

© Dale Sinclair, 2011

Published by RIBA Publishing, 15 Bonhill Street, London EC2P 2EA

ISBN 978 1 85946 392 5

Stock code 74336

The right of Dale Sinclair to be identified as the Author of this Work has been asserted in accordance with the Copyright, Design and Patents Act 1988.

All rights reserved. No part of this publication may be reproduced, stored in a retrieval system, or transmitted, in any form or by any means, electronic, mechanical, photocopying, recording or otherwise, without prior permission of the copyright owner.

British Library Cataloguing in Publications Data
A catalogue record for this book is available from the British Library.

Commissioning Editor: James Thompson
Project Editor: Alex Lazarou
Designed and typeset by Alex Lazarou
Printed and bound by Polestar Wheatons

While every effort has been made to check the accuracy and quality of the information given in this publication, neither the Author nor the Publisher accept any responsibility for the subsequent use of this information, for any errors or omissions that it may contain, or for any misunderstandings arising from it.

RIBA Publishing is part of RIBA Enterprises Ltd.
www.ribaenterprises.com

CONTENTS

CHAPTER 1
Introduction
1

CHAPTER 2
The Lead Consultant and Lead Designer: Managing Designers
5

CHAPTER 3
Co-ordination, Integration and Collaboration
19

CHAPTER 4
Programming Design
37

CHAPTER 5
Managing Cost
57

CHAPTER 6
Eight Essential Design Management Tools
73

CHAPTER 7
Reviewing Design
97

CHAPTER 8
How Procurement Affects the Design Management Challenge
109

CHAPTER 9
Streamlining Practice Management
117

CHAPTER 10
'Soft Skills'
129

Index
137

CHAPTER 1
INTRODUCTION

THE ENVIRONMENT in which architects work has changed. The three procurement mantras of time, cost and quality have now also become the three essential drivers for clients determining **who** designs their buildings:

- they want a design completed on **time** at each of the relevant stages;
- they want the design to be on **budget**; and
- they want an excellent design, delivered in line with their **quality** aspirations.

1.1 How do we respond to these drivers?

To respond to these demands and to ensure that all of these objectives are achieved, architects must now overlay management techniques onto their design processes. And, on top of this, the architect's workload is increasing and becoming ever-more diverse. The ability to produce a design on time and to budget is complicated by increased duties, such as those related to sustainability, disability and equality legislation or by obligations to co-ordinate the work of other designers or consultants.

While there are numerous books devoted to the subjects of architectural design and practice management, there are very few books devoted to the management of the architectural design process. In response, this book analyses the issues that have to be dealt with and then considers the most appropriate tools and techniques to manage the architectural design process.

In truth, many designers have the skills required to manage the design process. However, the intuitive way in which designers tend to make their decisions does not reveal the true complexity of the process and the extent to which they manage the other project consultants. By establishing at the outset the basis on which decisions are made,

LEADING THE TEAM

the design process becomes more transparent; any assumptions can be ratified and risks eliminated. More importantly, the client will understand the amount of work required in order to match their brief to a given site.

Any architect aspiring to become a great team leader needs simple and effective techniques to monitor the development of a project and the many issues which he/she is confronted with. More importantly, an architect needs these tools to demonstrate that they are on top of things and capable of handling greater responsibility on future projects.

In terms of leadership, the architect might have one or all of the following roles as:

- designer: leading the architectural design and delivering the 'vision';
- lead designer: managing the design process (and the other designers);
- lead consultant: managing design team issues associated with the design process;
- team leader: managing the architectural team.

This book focuses on the roles of lead designer and lead consultant, exploring what they entail, and considering along the way other related management issues that must be dealt with. On smaller projects, all four roles may be undertaken by one individual; however, as projects increase in size, and also as a result of the significant additional duties, these roles become specific and individual. On extremely large projects, there may be a number of individuals performing aspects of each role.

1.2 What is design management?

The process of formalising the management of the architectural design process is still in its embryonic stages and seems to be anathema to many architects. Perhaps this is due to the intuitive method of working that is derived from the long formal education process. In today's commercial environment, it is now clear that this informal, intuitive approach is no longer adequate to manage the many design issues that arise during a project. Architects must articulate the status of their designs, how they are managing project risks and how they are confirming any assumptions made during the early stages of the design.

To avoid any confusion regarding management terms, the typical meanings for project and design management are considered here.

KEY TERM **Project Management** is the discipline of planning, organising and managing resources to bring about the successful completion of specific project goals and objectives.

KEY TERM **Design Management** is the effective deployment by managers of the design resources available to an organisation in order to pursue its objectives.

From these, we can conclude that:

- project management concerns the overall management of a project and does not specifically deal with the management of the design process;
- design management is how organisations strategically use and harness design in order to achieve their goals.

If we reconsider the project management description and substitute 'design management' for 'project management' and 'the design process' for 'resources', we have:

Design Management is the discipline of planning, organising and managing the design process to bring about the successful completion of specific project goals and objectives.

This description may differ substantially from the definition of design management given above and, while some project managers may call this topic 'design project management', as it is effectively a management process overlaid on the design process, for the purposes of this book the term 'design management' will be used.

CHAPTER 2
THE LEAD CONSULTANT AND LEAD DESIGNER: MANAGING DESIGNERS

THE LEAD CONSULTANT AND LEAD DESIGNER, and the duties that they have to undertake, are central to the delivery of a successful project. This chapter considers the issues that must be navigated by the person undertaking these leadership roles. On the majority of projects, the architect is appointed lead consultant and lead designer. Exceptions might include projects with a substantial amount of engineering input, such as a major infrastructure project, where drivers might dictate that the civil engineering designer is better placed to lead the team.

The roles played by other designers, and how the allocation of design responsibility influences the design of a project, are also examined below.

2.1 Who, and what, needs to be managed?

New procurement routes, the increased use of project managers and shorter project timescales are recent trends which dictate a reshaping of these lead roles. Many different aspects of the process require management:

- More consultants are involved in projects. As well as the traditional designers (architectural, civil and structural engineering, building services), the cost consultant (sometimes referred to as the quantity surveyor) and the landscape architect, many specialist consultants have increased their project role and contributions. Other consultants include:
    - acoustic engineers
    - fire engineers

- sustainability advisers
- disability and access (DDA) advisers
- catering consultants.

All of these consultants have to be managed and their designs reviewed to ensure that they are co-ordinated with the work of the other designers prior to construction commencing.
- Contractor design (performance specified work) requires specialist subcontractors to produce design information. The timing of this design work creates significant design management issues as it is inevitable that it will be carried out concurrent with construction on site.
- More onerous appointment documents have emerged which increase design management duties. For example, the obligation to 'integrate' as well as 'co-ordinate' has resulted in greater responsibilities.
- In addition to leading the team, many clients require the lead consultant to employ the other designers (consultants), acting effectively as a 'one stop shop'. While this requirement might not change the design process, in practice it has significant contractual and legal implications.

In summary, there are now a greater number of designers involved in any given project. Their contributions have to be carefully managed and co-ordinated. As the lead consultant may have to accept full responsibility for all of the designers and the lead designer must co-ordinate the work of more designers and specialist subcontractors, these roles have clearly increased in complexity. This chapter considers the implications that these issues have for those leading the team.

2.2 What are the key management roles on a project?

In addition to the role of designers (architectural, civil and structural engineering and building services), the cost consultant and the CDM co-ordinator, there are a number of other roles that need to be undertaken in order to deliver a project successfully. These are succinctly set out in the schedule of role specifications in the RIBA appointment and include the:

- project manager
- contract administrator/employer's agent
- lead consultant
- lead designer.

The project manager's role is to act as the main interface with the client and to manage the project team, a role that does not require a significant interface with the design process, or designing, per se. The contract administrator/employer's agent role deals with the management of the tender process and the administration of the building contract and need not involve a direct interface with the design process, although the individual undertaking this role may also be one of the designers. As these roles do not directly relate to the management of the design process they are not covered in detail in this book.

What are the duties of the lead consultant and lead designer?

The lead consultant and lead designer roles are integral to the design process and, in order to consider how best to lead a design team, we must first consider best practice for carrying out these roles. By differentiating between the lead consultant and the lead designer, the client has a degree of flexibility when determining who is best placed to undertake these roles, although on the vast majority of projects one consultant will be appointed to undertake both roles. The lead consultant role is more management-orientated and does not necessarily have to be undertaken by a designer. The lead designer's role requires design skills and, more importantly, any practice or individual undertaking this role would need to have the relevant professional qualifications and professional indemnity insurance.

The architect has historically been the leader of the design team. While one practice, and one individual, may typically undertake both the lead consultant and lead designer roles, there is significant value in differentiating between the management processes that each role entails in order to ensure that a successful design is developed (role of lead designer) and the processes directly related to design activities and decisions (role of lead consultant).

In the rare circumstances that the architect does not undertake the lead consultant role but performs the lead designer role, he/she may still wish to allocate a team leader who will deal with the management duties that the lead consultant is not undertaking. These would typically be the management of the appointment process, the management of resources or other activities not directly related to the design process but without which the design process would not be efficient or would result in too many risks to a business.

On larger projects, the different nature of directing the work of other designers and directing the design process can result in the need for two individuals to manage the different aspects of a project.

LEADING THE TEAM

The duties expected of the lead consultant and lead designer, as defined by the RIBA Agreements 2010, are set out below along with the chapter in which that specific duty is discussed.

What are the lead consultant's duties?

DUTY (emphasis added)	RELEVANT CHAPTER
Advising on the need for and the scope of services by consultants, specialists, subcontractors or suppliers	See Chapter 2
Facilitating communications between the client and consultants except that communications on significant design matters are dealt with by the Lead Designer and/or the CDM Co-ordinator	See Chapter 9
Leading and co-ordination, preparation of a project quality plan, and **work stage programmes**, including **work outstanding from previous stages**	See Chapter 3
Advising on methods of procuring construction	See Chapter 8
Monitoring the work of the consultants	See Chapter 2
Reviewing the progress of design work in conjunction with the Lead Designer and CDM Co-ordinator	See Chapter 3
Developing and managing change control procedures, and making or obtaining decisions necessary for time and cost control	See Chapter 5
Receiving regular status reports from each consultant including the Design Leader, CDM Co-ordinator and Contract Administrator/Employer's Agent	See Chapter 3
With the Contract Administrator, the Lead Designer and the CDM Co-ordinator, **co-ordinating and reviewing the work of consultants** and site inspectors **after stage G**	See Chapter 3 and Chapter 8
Issuing instructions reasonably necessary for the purpose of time and cost control or co-ordination of design work within the scope of the Project subject to obtaining prior approval of the Client	See Chapter 5
Reporting to the Client at regular intervals **on progress** or, as necessary, applying for further instructions or approval to proceed	See Chapter 4

CHAPTER 2 MANAGING DESIGNERS

What are the lead designer's duties?

DUTY (emphasis added)	RELEVANT CHAPTER
Co-ordinating preparation of work stage programme(s) for the design process	See Chapter 3
Co-ordinating design of all constructional elements, including work by consultants, specialists or suppliers **and for health and safety matters** in conjunction with the CDM Co-ordinator	See Chapter 7
Establishing the form and content of **design outputs, their interfaces and a verification procedure**	See Chapter 3
Communicating with the Client on **significant** design issues	See Chapter 10

2.3 Design team structure

Having considered the duties of the lead consultant and lead designer in the previous section, this section considers their relationship with the client and other designers. These relationships are critical as they can affect a party's ability to direct and manage and, depending on the nature of the relationship, may also present additional risks to their practice(s).

In a 'traditional' design team structure, all design team members are appointed directly by the client as illustrated in Figure 2.1.

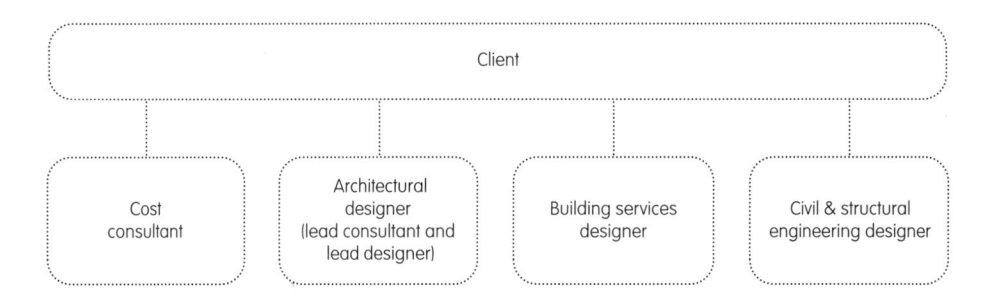

```
                            Client
        ┌──────────────┬──────────────┬──────────────┐
                    Architectural
       Cost          designer        Building services    Civil & structural
    consultant    (lead consultant and    designer       engineering designer
                   lead designer)
```

FIGURE 2.1: Client appointed design team

Even with the shift in procurement trends towards design and build, clients still generally tend to appoint each consultant directly although it is common for these appointments to be novated to the contractor (this is discussed further in Chapter 9).

Increasingly, as an alternative to the client-appointed team, the lead consultant is requested to employ the design team (the designers) as subconsultants. This option is attractive to clients as it enables them to deal with just one consultant and avoids their involvement in any disputes which may arise between the designers.

In these situations, the architect generally assembles the design team and assumes the role of lead consultant, lead designer and architectural designer. When assembling a team in response to an invitation to tender, it is likely that the architect will already know the other designers being asked to join the team and, typically, will have worked with them previously. If the bid is successful the architect will then directly employ these designers as subconsultants. With such a team, the contractual lines change, as illustrated in Figure 2.2.

CHAPTER 2 MANAGING DESIGNERS

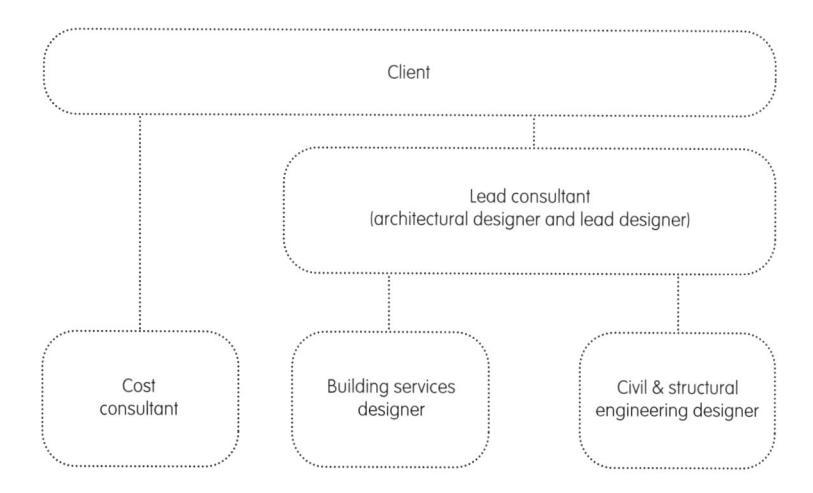

FIGURE 2.2: Lead designer appointed design team

In this scenario, although the day-to-day working relationships within the team are the same as in the case of client-appointed designers, this contractual relationship creates significant additional risks to the lead consultant's practice.

From the client's perspective, there are various pros and cons in the lead consultant employing the design team:

- The client only needs to deal with a single party and does not have to manage a number of relationships.
- The chemistry between the team members is likely to be better as the parties have not been brought together in an 'arranged marriage'.
- An established team is likely to have developed good and efficient working relationships.
- If the client has a dispute regarding any aspect of the services, the lead consultant becomes responsible for all of the design and is the single point of responsibility.
- In the event of a dispute between the individual designers, the client is no longer party to that dispute. The consultants must resolve any disagreements among themselves.

The downside, from the client's position, might include the following factors:

- A combined team bid may not be as competitive as the client is no longer able to negotiate each individual fee and appointment.
- If the client dislikes or has had a poor experience with one of the designers in the team, it can be difficult to change that consultant.

Managing the risks in a client-appointed team

Although no project is without its issues, when each designer proactively and efficiently carries out their duties, a project tends to run smoothly. However, when one or more of the designers fail to provide the services required of them, additional co-ordination and management time has to be expended. While appointment documents set out the lead consultant's and lead designer's duties in relation to managing and co-ordinating other designers, they remain silent on what processes should take place should these designers fail to perform as required or expected, requiring additional management time to be spent:

- carrying out numerous reviews of drawings, or other information, as a result of other designers not taking due notice of agreements or decisions made in meetings, workshops or in relation to comments made on drawings (this is covered in detail in Chapter 7: Reviewing design);
- organising and attending meetings with the designers to resolve ongoing co-ordination issues. Failure to resolve such issues quickly may also have a knock-on effect on other designers' work and, as the design progresses, this may greatly impact a significant number of drawings; or
- resolving co-ordination issues that arise on site.

The lead designer can find that those designers who are employed and paid by the client do not respond to their requests or instructions. While such examples may be rare, it is essential to consider what measures might assist in the management of such designers.

In order to manage these risks, the lead consultant may need to:

- obtain copies of each designer's appointment at the start of the project;
- highlight and address any anomalies or contradictions with the lead consultant's own duties;
- ensure that the project quality plan is prepared, agreed by all parties and includes the agreed stage deliverables;
- use monthly project reports to set out the status of each designer's progress and to list any problems that are being encountered;
- ensure that his/her own internal team reports any problems so that appropriate representations can be made to the other designers' senior management;

- hold monthly principals' meetings (particularly on larger projects). These can act as a useful forum for addressing issues and dealing with any broader political issues or 'hot topics'; and
- as a last resort, and to protect his/her own position, write to the client to advise that they are unable to perform the duties of lead consultant as a result of another consultant failing to fulfil their duties.

If applicable, the lead designer should set out the specific elements of design that other designers are failing to deliver and the implications of this failure on the lead designer's co-ordination duties; or, conversely, set out the aspects that he/she believes will not be co-ordinated as a result of a specific designer's inadequate service.

KEY TERM   **Consultant** other designers can also be referred to as consultants and, in line with the RIBA appointment documents, both terms are used throughout this book, depending on the situation.

KEY TERM   **Subconsultant** this term is preferred by designers as it distinguishes the subconsultant from the subcontractors employed by a contractor. In some instances, subconsultants may be referred to as subcontractors. This is also correct as work is being subcontracted to the consultant.

What are the risks when the lead consultant appoints the team?

The benefits to the lead consultant include the ability to:

- select consultants with which to work;
- work with designers with similar processes, culture and approaches to design;
- assemble a team that has an established track record, creating a stronger bid;
- manage other designers, being in the position of employer; and
- continually improve the team's project processes, using knowledge and feedback from previous projects.

LEADING THE TEAM

There are, however, numerous additional risks:

- the lead consultant's bid costs increase as other designers' contributions have to be co-ordinated, and possibly reformatted, to provide a holistic bid;
- the lead consultant is contractually responsible for the performance of the other designers (the subconsultants);
- the lead consultant is responsible for paying the invoices of the subconsultants, regardless of whether he/she has been paid by the client;
- the lead consultant needs to put subcontracts (appointments) with the other designers in place; and
- the success of the team's bid could be jeopardised if one of the designers has submitted a fee that is not competitive.

How can these additional risks be managed?

While there are certain advantages in submitting bids as a predetermined design team, the significant additional risks must be identified and carefully managed. Ways of achieving this include:

- the careful selection of consultants;
- establishing subconsultant appointments;
- the considered compilation of fee proposals;
- monitoring of invoicing from, and payments to, subconsultants;
- developing integrated working methods; and
- monitoring the performance of subconsultants.

Selecting consultants wisely

The basis for selecting consultants should be straightforward, based on the following considerations:

- Who have you recently worked with on similar projects?
- Was the relationship successful?
- Do the consultants have a good track record in the relevant sector?
- Is their design approach compatible with your own?
- Will the consultants be entering into an exclusive agreement to be part of your bid team or do they intend to participate in another bid? (If it is

not possible to obtain an exclusive agreement, it is important to consider confidentiality issues. For example, consider using separate offices of the same consultant.)

Correctly appointing subconsultants

In preparing the bid, the proposed subconsultants need to be made aware of and allowed to comment on any appointment documents proposed by the client. If a bid is successful, the lead consultant must appoint the other designers using a formal appointment process, including a consultation on the appointment being agreed with the client to ensure that they can accept the terms. This will help to ensure that all subconsultant appointments are 'back-to-back' with the lead consultant's own appointment. If a practice is subcontracting work to the same subconsultants on a regular basis, there are benefits in establishing a framework agreement.

Whatever arrangement is agreed, it is essential that any subconsultant appointments be concluded and signed within the same timeframe as the lead consultant's appointment with the client. Failure to resolve a subconsultant's appointment could create significant risks, should the client have an issue with an element of the services performed by that subconsultant.

Getting the fee proposal right

The competitiveness of a team bid relies on all members of the team putting forward their best price. Any consultant assembling a team should consider how best to benchmark the fees from the various proposed subconsultants to ensure they are competitive. Such benchmarking might also reveal fees which are too low, potentially leading to issues later on in the project if the subconsultant fails to provide the services set out in the appointment.

When assembling a team, it may be difficult for the lead consultant to add a mark-up to the fees of the other designers as this will be counterproductive to the submission of a competitive bid. However, the position is different where the client or project manager requests that the lead designer employs another designer. In this situation it is reasonable for the lead consultant to add a management fee, on top of the subconsultant's fee, to cover the additional risks and management duties.

Monitoring payments to subconsultants

Payments to subconsultants will be made by the lead consultant, who needs to appreciate that if the client fails to pay promptly the subconsultants will still seek payment under the terms of their agreements, regardless of the payment situation with the client. The implications for a practice's cash flow could be significant if a major consultant with substantial fees, such as the civil and structural (C&S) engineering consultant, seeks prompt payment prior to the lead consultant being paid by the client.

This dictates a much more stringent approach to vetting potential clients and the lead consultant should investigate the financial stability and corporate structure of a client before entering into a contract. For example, has a special purpose vehicle (SPV) been established for a specific project? A less tolerant attitude to late payment might also be essential and the services of subconsultant designers may need to be suspended if payment periods become protracted.

On a day-to-day basis, subconsultants will pursue the lead consultant's accounts department for payment and their invoices will be dealt with by the lead consultant's accounting systems. The status of subconsultant fee drawdowns requires constant monitoring, and accruals may be needed where invoicing has not yet taken place. The risks and work involved in these 'behind the scenes' invoicing and cash flow issues should not be underestimated.

Establishing integrated working methods

If a team is regularly working together, bids can be strengthened by setting out the processes that have been used to successfully deliver previous projects. Chapter 9 discusses continual improvement and feedback in relation to a practice, but the same techniques can be applied to a design team.

Regardless, bids are stronger when the team can demonstrate in their proposals that they have integrated procedures and processes in place and where they have set out the benefits and added value that these will bring to the project. Workshops to discuss project processes will not only result in a stronger bid but, by learning from previous experiences, future projects can be run more effectively and efficiently.

Monitoring performance

The techniques set out above for managing poorly performing consultants employed by the client are equally valid for managing subconsultants. However, it should be remembered that once subconsultants are appointed, the lead consultant is liable for their performance and for the design information that they issue.

In the event of a dispute arising from the services of a subconsultant it should be noted that the client will claim against the lead consultant's professional indemnity insurance (PII) policy, and that their insurers will then make a claim against the subconsultant's policy. Resolving multi-party disputes can be complex and difficult, and it is best to attempt to settle any disputes outside court as costs could quickly escalate.

And what about the cost consultants?

While it is increasingly common for clients to request full team bids, which include the M&E and C&S designers as well as the other peripheral designers, the cost consultant is still generally appointed directly by the client (see Figure 2.2 above). Where a bid requires a cost consultant to be part of the lead consultant's team, a further layer of risks needs to be considered:

- What happens if any of the subconsultants have to redesign as a result of an error in the cost plan?
- How does the lead consultant check the cost allowances for the other designers?

When appointing the cost consultant, the lead consultant should also consider how the cost plan can be benchmarked against previous project data or other industry-wide information. This, along with other methods for managing cost, are covered further in Chapter 5: Managing cost.

Conclusion to Chapter 2
The Lead Consultant and Lead Designer: Managing Designers

ONE   The lead consultant and lead designer roles are typically undertaken by a single party, but there are benefits in considering the duties of each role separately.

TWO   The client or lead consultant will be accepting different risks that need to be managed differently depending on which party has employed the other designers.

THREE   If the lead consultant employs the other designers he/she must consider how to manage the significant additional risks that arise.

CHAPTER 3
CO-ORDINATION, INTEGRATION AND COLLABORATION

IN THE FOLLOWING CHAPTERS we will consider the techniques that the lead consultant or lead designer might use to manage the design process. Before considering these, it is essential to consider the contribution that other designers make to the design process as their design work creates the greatest design management challenges. Here, we will examine the risks associated with any co-ordination obligations that the lead consultant and lead designer may have. We then examine the issues associated with managing contractor design elements of a project and how these are integrated into the co-ordinated design.

The successful co-ordination and integration of the design work from many designers requires exemplary teamwork and a collaborative effort. We conclude this chapter by examining potential obstacles to such working practices and how these can be overcome.

3.1 Co-ordination

The last chapter clarified that the lead consultant and lead designer are required to co-ordinate various aspects of the project. From a liability perspective, co-ordination presents significant risks to those undertaking the duty to co-ordinate, partly due to its loose definition (see below), but mainly because the outputs of a co-ordinated design come from different designers who:

- in the majority of instances, are not employed by the lead consultant or designer;
- have not been selected or vetted by the lead consultant or lead designer;
- may not previously have worked with the lead consultant or lead designer;

- are still ultimately responsible for their own design work; or
- may be designing during the construction period.

On site, co-ordination issues are probably among the biggest discussion topics yet it is difficult to obtain an adequate definition of 'co-ordinate' or 'co-ordination' specific to the work of the lead consultant or lead designer. This needs to be considered before methods of co-ordinating can be determined. A typical dictionary definition provides us with a useful starting point:

KEY TERM   **Co-ordinate** to work together harmoniously.

KEY TERM   **Co-ordination** the act of co-ordinating, making all aspects work together for a common goal or purpose.

The co-ordination duties in the RIBA appointment (listed in Chapter 2) are generally **tasks** such as 'co-ordinates preparation of work stage programme(s) for the design process' or 'co-ordinates design of all constructional elements'. However, bespoke appointments may contain more onerous requirements with respect to the **outputs** from these tasks, such as 'a co-ordinated design' or a 'co-ordinated programme'.

'Co-ordinate' vs 'co-ordinated' – more than a grammatical difference

The difference between tasks and outputs is very subtle but quite different responsibilities are created. For example, to 'co-ordinate the preparation of a work stage programme' requires the lead consultant to obtain information from the relevant parties (designers, client and possibly third parties, such as planning or utility companies) and to produce a programme using this information.

The obligation to produce a 'co-ordinated programme' is far more onerous and, indeed, may not be achievable. For example, when a programme is prepared using the periods requested by each party it may exceed the timescale allocated by the project manager. In these circumstances, it could be said that the lead consultant has co-ordinated the inputs with the other designers, but that the programme is not co-ordinated.

Equally, from the lead designer's perspective, the requirement to 'co-ordinate design' is

CHAPTER 3 CO-ORDINATION, INTEGRATION AND COLLABORATION

less onerous than the requirement to produce 'a co-ordinated design'. For example, a discussion at a design workshop may conclude how a specific design aspect is to be developed: the C&S and M&E engineering aspects of a plantroom, for example. The minutes of the workshop might record how the design was co-ordinated but one of the designers, say the M&E designers, may not have incorporated the agreed approach into their design, for whatever reason. The lead designer can demonstrate that the obligation to 'co-ordinate design' was discharged (the minutes) but, as the M&E designer's drawings will not correlate with the lead designer's own, there is not a co-ordinated design.

It is important to dwell on these differences and more so to consider how the lead consultant or lead designer can demonstrate that they have successfully fulfilled any co-ordination duties. The stage at which the work of other designers is reviewed is also critical and this is discussed further below.

One obstacle to co-ordinating design, and the production of co-ordinated information, is that there is no single document that defines **precisely** what each designer should produce at each RIBA design stage. To make matters still more difficult, the generic professional appointment documents for mechanical and electrical services (M&E) and civil and structural engineering (C&S) are not specifically aligned to the RIBA design stages and have differing and ambiguous guidance in terms of co-ordination. To resolve this conundrum, four items need to be considered:

1. **Iterative design**
   Chapter 4 discusses the process of iterative design and the difficulties of programming the early design stages, along with potential methods of resolving these.
2. **General arrangement (GA) drawings**
   Successful development of the general arrangement drawings (plans, sections and elevations) is pivotal to successful co-ordination. They must, however, develop incrementally. The items that the lead designer should conclude by each stage are listed below. By adhering to this list, these crucial drawings will progress in line with any programme constraints. The use of 3D files in lieu of 2D general arrangement drawings is also becoming more common and is discussed further in the collaborative working section at the end of this chapter although the same principles apply.
3. **Design status**
   Each designer's information develops from its preliminary nature to tender status and, ultimately, to contract or construction status, when the design is

used to construct elements on site or for use by a subcontractor to produce their own design work (contractor design). If abortive construction work or contractor design is to be avoided, the designer's construction information needs to be as accurate as possible and one of the key challenges of co-ordination is considering what inputs each designer requires, and when, in order to achieve this. For example, if the structural engineer has to produce construction information for a plantroom he/she will require finalised and accurate information on trenches, pits and plinths. The lead consultant and designer must therefore determine who will provide this and when. Design status is covered further in the design dependency section in Chapter 4. It is probably true to say that many of the co-ordination issues encountered on site relate to clashes between structure and services, and managing the co-ordination of these aspects is therefore an important task.

4. **Consultant appointments**

   At the start of the project it is imperative that the lead designer ensures that the deliverables of all designers at each stage are defined and are sufficient for him/her to co-ordinate the design or to achieve a co-ordinated design. If this is not the case, any issue should be addressed with the client, and the relevant designer(s), and the agreed deliverables included in the project quality plan.

3.2 What co-ordination work should take place at each RIBA stage?

Stage C – Concept

It is essential to remember that, while the focus of stage C is the creation of a concept, the GA drawings that are produced must also demonstrate that the design has been developed to take account of the work of the other designers. To achieve this, the outline proposals that are required should, fundamentally, be about strategy and not detail. Undertaking the following at the end of stage C will provide a springboard to the design co-ordination that will occur at stage D:

- **Civil and structural engineering (C&S) designer**
  - Analysis of ground conditions, possible substructure and foundation options and recommendations for the most appropriate solution. This might include how different grids or structures will influence the substructure and foundation solution.

- Typical bay drawings, showing the different grid options that have been considered with the architectural designer and different structural solutions that have been investigated for the main frame. No conclusions should be drawn as other factors may determine the selection and the lead designer's report should summarise these.
- Sketch details for any specialist structures that may be required (for example, atriums or entrances).
- **Mechanical and electrical services (M&E) designer**
  - The M&E engineer should set out initial strategies for the various systems in the building and should have produced a plantroom and riser schedule early enough in the process to allow the areas required to be shown on the GA drawings.
- **Architectural designer**
  - GA drawings showing a grid that matches one of the options produced by the C&S designer and plantrooms and major risers that tie in with the plantroom and riser schedule shown on the M&E drawings or schedule.

In the early stages of a project, the lead designer needs to provide design leadership and ensure that the principles of the M&E and C&S designs are properly thought through and co-ordinated with the architectural design. If the information indicated above is produced, the outline cost plan should contain adequate allowances for the mechanical services and structural engineering elements of the scheme and the ground work for the design development stage (Stage D) will have been adequately prepared. To attempt to do any more than this will be counterproductive to the design process and to produce any less will result in fundamental co-ordination aspects being considered at the commencement of stage D.

Stage D – Design development

During this stage, the majority of high-level co-ordination work must be undertaken if significant abortive work is to be avoided in the preparation of tender information. The outline proposals and typical bays developed at stage C should be progressed and, if the appropriate design development work has been undertaken at stage C, the key objectives of stage D will be to consider items such as:

- developed riser locations, dimensions and access requirements;
- more detailed plantroom configurations including escape provisions and access for maintenance;

- louvre requirements, flue locations or other M&E elements that impact on the external envelope;
- how structural bracing will be incorporated into the design; or
- strategies for all mechanical and electrical services including access considerations.

Workshops are the most effective means of moving forward co-ordination issues and the means of successfully running these workshops is discussed further in Chapter 6: Eight essential design management tools. If the above items have been properly considered, the next level of co-ordination will have been undertaken and the cost plan will also take cognisance of this work.

Stage E – Technical design

The objective at the end of stage E should be a set of architectural GA drawings that have been completed in sufficient detail to enable each designer to commence with the preparation of their own production information. The iterative design process should now be complete. Specifically, these drawings should include:

- finalised plantroom configurations and locations signed off by the M&E designer;
- finalised riser configurations and locations signed off by the M&E designer;
- finalised stair and lift locations checked for building control compliance; and
- typical architect's details for the building envelope that show grid lines, column and slab positions.

To achieve these objectives the C&S and M&E engineers should have progressed the relevant detailed aspects of their own GA drawings as well as assisted with the development of key co-ordination aspects which, in turn, will have helped to ensure that their own drawings are aligned with the architectural GA drawings.

The key point at this stage is ensuring that the detail used to create the GA drawings will not change or, if it does, that the reasons are clear and that the timing of the resolution of any residual issues is clear to all parties. Lift shafts are a good example. Have they been designed to British Standards (BS) or to suit the standard sizes available from a number of manufacturers? Will fixing the shaft size result in additional tender costs? Or, can a way of adapting the shaft, later in the design process to suit the successful lift manufacturer, be agreed? The design status schedule should record any such decisions, especially if they require future design work or become tender constraints.

Stage F1 – Production information (for tender purposes)

With the iterative process complete at the end of stage E, the work of each designer should focus on their own design aspects during this stage. Co-ordination issues will still arise but can be dealt with at regular workshops.

Co-ordination work should now concern the detail and should not impact on the GA drawings.

Stage F2 – Production information (for construction purposes)

While it is unlikely that the issue of production information to site will impact on co-ordination that has been undertaken to date, it is possible that the design work of specialist subcontractors will impact on aspects that have already been co-ordinated. This is considered further in the section on design dependencies in Chapter 4: Programming design.

The key co-ordination consideration at this stage will be the reviewing of other designer's (C&S and M&E) drawings before they are issued for construction. This is an obligation on the lead designer who has, according to the RIBA appointment, the duty of *'Co-ordinating design of all constructional elements, including work by consultants, specialists or suppliers' and 'establishing ... a verification procedure'*.

One critical point to consider is that, although the lead designer will have used a number of methods to co-ordinate the design prior to tender (as set out above), time constraints normally prevent a review of this information (although, if there is an obligation to produce a co-ordinated design, it is essential that a review is carried out). Once the lead designer has reviewed the information, he/she should consider the nature of any comments as it is possible that a building contract will be in place and that comments may have cost implications. If so, they should be dealt with using the change control mechanism. This is considered further in Chapter 5 and also in Chapter 7: Reviewing design.

How can a high degree of co-ordination be achieved?

With the outputs for each stage determined, we can consider the steps that the lead designer should take to ensure that these are achieved, for example:

- allocate a member of the team to focus on the work of the other designers to ensure that they can produce their design inputs in time to be incorporated into the architectural GA drawings (this can be a significant challenge if a change in the concept emerges late in the stage C process);
- hold focused workshops with the appropriate designers present: it is beneficial to hold such workshops in each designer's office in turn so that the lead designer can speak to all of the designers in their own environment. The best decision making and problem solving happens face to face. The lead designer also needs to ensure that design decisions agreed in these workshops are adequately recorded; and
- review the information of the other designers. Although this is not strictly an obligation until construction information is produced, the review of other designers' information is an essential part of the co-ordination process. Where timescales do not allow this to occur (see further in Chapter 4: Programming design), the marking up of ad hoc prints at the other consultants' offices can at least allow the review process to commence.

3.3 Integration

If the co-ordination process set out above has been adhered to, the design information of the various designers should be co-ordinated when it is issued for construction. However, though the design work of the design team has been substantially completed when all their construction information has been issued, it is highly likely that there will be elements of contractor design contained in the building contract that will need further consideration.

In some consultant appointments this is referred to as integrating the design work of other designers and, while this term does not appear in the RIBA appointment, which requires that the lead consultant '*co-ordinates design of all constructional elements including work by consultants, specialist or suppliers*', it is common for bespoke appointments to include obligations such as 'integrate into the design of the project any requirements of specialist consultants or contractors'.

KEY TERM **Integrate** to bring together or incorporate (parts) into a whole.

CHAPTER 3 CO-ORDINATION, INTEGRATION AND COLLABORATION

KEY TERM   **Contractor design** historically, it was typical practice for designers to nominate specialist subcontractors as part of the design and procurement process. This allowed designers to develop details with specialist(s) **during** the preparation of the tender information and resulted in the design information of specialists being fully co-ordinated into the design at an early stage. However, new procurement routes and standard form of contract have fundamentally changed the way that specialist subcontractors engage with the design process. The benefits of contractor design and the means of determining the extent of contractor design are set out below, but it is essential for designers to consider that this later involvement in the design process results in the overlap of design and construction and that this creates significant design management risks, particularly in relation to some of the obligations that designers may have in their appointments, and that a number of design processes need to be considered to manage the associated design risks.

In some construction contracts, contractor design is defined as **Performance Specified Work** and, where this term is used, the points raised in relation to contractor design have the same validity. This term derives from the use of performance specifications where work is specified descriptively instead of prescriptively.

In certain instances there is a fine line between what the consultant designs and what the contractor designs. For example, the architect may specify toilet cubicles and will draw these on his GA drawings. However, it is commonplace and necessary for the subcontractor who is installing this work to produce 'shop drawings' to enable the various components to be manufactured (sometimes this work will be undertaken by the supplier on behalf of an approved installer). This type of drawing work is not deemed to be contractor design and in some instances such drawings will not be issued to the designers for review. For clarity, when the **Design Responsibility Matrix** (one of the eight essential design tools – see Chapter 6) is being developed, it can be useful to list such elements so that there are no ambiguities about which aspects of the design the designers intend to review.

A contractor who provides the design, manufacturing and installation of a particular aspect of the construction is typically called a **Specialist Subcontractor** and would usually be appointed by a main contractor as a domestic subcontractor. In some forms of procurement the appointment may be made as a **Trade Contractor** or **Works Contractor**. Although the term 'contractor design' is frequently used, it is highly likely that this design work will be undertaken by a subcontractor. However, in design and build forms of procurement the contractor will be responsible for all aspects of the design, including the design work of the consultants. The impact that procurement has on design responsibility is covered in greater detail in Chapter 8.

Not surprisingly, if the design work of specialist contractors is to be successfully integrated into the design, the co-ordinated design must have taken account of as many known design factors as possible and a number of assumptions will have been made. In this section we now consider the four key areas that designers, and those leading and managing the design, need to consider in relation to the integration of contractor design.

1   Extent of contractor design

Early on in the design process, ideally before the end of stage D, the design team, led by the lead consultant and the lead designer, needs to determine what aspects of the design will be designed by the contractor. This is crucial for a number of reasons:

- the design drawings and specifications must be developed in either a prescriptive or descriptive manner (covered in greater detail below);
- the extent of contractor design needs to be clear in the tender issue to enable contractors tendering for a project to provide for the costs of undertaking any such design work;
- it must be clear to the lead designer what aspects of other designers' work will not be completed at tender stage so that any assumptions made concerning co-ordination work can be stated in the tender; and
- the client or project manager may also have their own views on what elements should be contractor design and they should therefore also be involved in the decision-making process.

CHAPTER 3 CO-ORDINATION, INTEGRATION AND COLLABORATION

The extent of contractor design will vary from project to project, depending on the views of the contributing parties and the nature of the design. Deciding on the elements of a project that should be contractor design is not straightforward, but advantages include that:

- a number of systems for a given situation can be considered, ensuring best value for the client;
- different installers, who may utilise different systems or have their own bespoke system, can tender for a project; and
- in more specialist situations, specialist subcontractors can utilise their unique design and manufacturing skills, thereby allowing the 'collective' of designers to produce a more cost-effective and integrated design.

Conversely, be aware that:

- aspects of the design are still being developed during the construction process and may impact on elements that have already been constructed or on co-ordinated design information that has been issued for construction;
- designers need to produce design intent drawings and then review the design and fabrication drawings of the subcontractor as well as integrating aspects of these designs that might change their own design intent information, particularly at the interfaces with other elements.

Once the extent of contractor design has been agreed by all of the relevant parties it can be recorded in a schedule (there are no industry standards for this although it might be called a 'design responsibility matrix') and tender information can then be produced in accordance with this schedule. The contents of this matrix are considered further in Chapter 6: Eight essential design management tools.

2 Performance specifications

Traditional specification methods that involve specifying in a prescriptive manner are not suitable for contractor design elements where items need to be specified descriptively to give the contractor flexibility to select appropriate products that meet certain standards. Performance specifications provide these standards. The two brief specification descriptions below illustrate the rigid nature of a standard, or prescriptive specification, and the greater flexibility that a descriptive clause offers in allowing the specialist to choose or design elements that meet the relevant standards.

29

EXAMPLE   **Prescriptive specification clause** mill finish standing seam roof at 300 mm centres, fixed to structural liner tray using proprietary clips ref 123, on 150 mm deep mineral wool insulation on manufacturer Y's structural tray ref. ABCD, 150 mm deep, on 262 mm deep galvanised steel purlins fixed to steel beams at 6,000 mm centres.

EXAMPLE   **Descriptive specification clause** mill finish standing seam roof at 300 mm centres, insulated to conform to the current building regulations and in general to specification section X.X, fixed back to the steel frame (as detailed on structural engineer's drawings).

Determining the scope of contractor design elements by the end of stage D allows specifications to be developed using descriptive or prescriptive clauses. However, to complicate matters, it should be noted that some prescriptive elements, which will not be designed by the contractor, may also have descriptive clauses. Examples include:

- ceiling systems, which can be specified prescriptively with the support system specified descriptively and determined by the installer on site;
- brickwork elements, which can be designed prescriptively but with certain components (such as wall ties) specified descriptively to allow the contractor to select the most cost-effective components from its own supply chain in accordance with the relevant specification clauses.

In these instances, the descriptive elements relate to elements that will be concealed in the final construction and this form of specifying allows the contractor to exercise discretion in applying construction skills and expertise, or utilising established supply chain relationships, in determining what components to use or how best to construct a specific aspect of the design. Similarly, a designer might specify descriptively yet insert into the specification products that the designer considers would meet the criteria. This gives the contractor a general direction, but leaves open the final decision on how to proceed. Finally, 'or similar and approved' is still utilised in certain prescriptive specifications to enable the contractor, or their subcontractors, to put forward alternative products. However, it should be noted that the designer does not have to agree to such products and, on the basis that accepting such changes may involve the designer in significant research yet create savings for the contractor, it is reasonable that a fee is agreed for reviewing such proposed changes. More importantly, designers need to remember that once they have agreed to changes they will be liable for the products used. Therefore, if they have any doubts regarding such alternatives, they should say so.

3   Design intent drawings

With designers unable to **finalise** the design of contractor design elements prior to tender, a means of developing the design for co-ordination and tender purposes is required. Design intent information enables the principles of the contractor design elements to be drawn, allowing them to be developed in parallel with other aspects of the design. This approach also:

- communicates the design concept to the tendering specialists, allowing them to develop those elements as part of their tender proposals;
- clarifies the scope of the anticipated works in sufficient detail to ensure that accurate tender costs are submitted;
- enables zones to be established to allow the structure and other aspects to be developed in parallel; and
- allows adjacent interfaces to be considered and set out. For example, allowing brickwork to proceed on site while the curtain walling is being tendered.

There is little guidance available on what design intent drawings should contain, but in the preparation of this information designers should meet with specialist subcontractors, who will be tendering for this portion of the work, to enable as many design aspects as possible to be considered in the preparation of tender 'design intent' information. As the design will be developed in detail by the specialist subcontractor, the designer should be careful not to draw too much detail as this may limit the ability of the specialist to contribute to the design or may confer responsibility on the designer for areas that require design skills which he/she does not possess. Conversely, if too little is drawn, particularly at interfaces, co-ordination with other aspects of the work may not be adequately achieved. The typical content for an element for which the architect is responsible is shown in Figure 3.1 and an element for which a specialist subcontractor will develop the proposals is illustrated in Figure 3.2.

It is inevitable that assumptions will have to be made and that aspects of the design will change once a specialist subcontractor is appointed and has completed the design. The design status schedule referred to in the previous paragraph can record these assumptions and may also allow the contractor to consider what aspects of design may have an impact on the construction programme.

LEADING THE TEAM

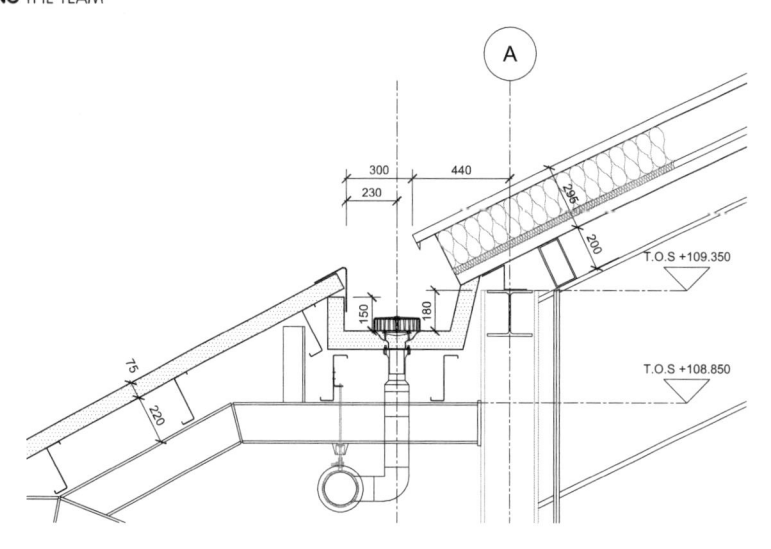

FIGURE 3.1: Architect design

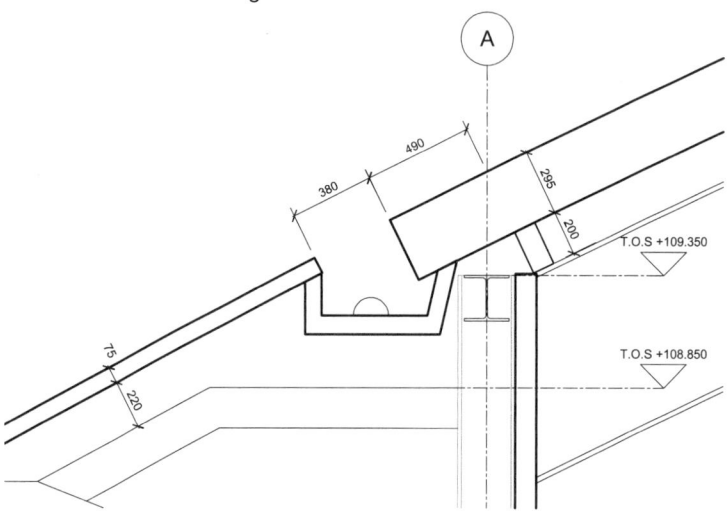

FIGURE 3.2: Architect design intent for contractor design

By considering construction aspects, designers can provide a significant contribution to the contractor by drawing attention to areas where specialist contractor design work will not be completed in line with the programme or where the interfaces between elements may impact work being carried out on site. Chapter 4: Programming design considers this in detail, along with the subject of design dependency.

One issue to which designers need to be alert is that, while design intent drawings will still be issued 'for construction' to allow the specialist subcontractors to develop their design, the specialist contractors' approved drawings will eventually supersede these drawings. This is discussed further in Chapter 7: Reviewing design.

4 Package design

In order to allow design, procurement and construction to occur simultaneously, management contracting requires that each element of the building is allocated to a specialist subcontractor. While the management contractor will produce package scope documents, the designers should consider that they could assist in this process, subject to the relevant fees being paid, by:

- issuing drawings defining the specific scope of work for each specialist subcontractor (shading of elevations for example);
- issuing package specifications that assist in clarifying the scope and setting out the detailed constraints for each package; and
- showing package reference numbers for each element on detail drawings, paying particular attention to interfaces. For example, is the brickwork or curtain walling trade contractor installing the mastic between the brickwork and curtain walling?

While some argue that certain of these tasks are the responsibility of the management contractor, there is no doubt that a co-ordinated set of designers' drawings and specifications, aligned with the management contractor's scope documents, will lead to fewer claims and disputes from subcontractors. It can also be argued that producing package information for a design and build (D&B) or private finance initiative (PFI) contractor would also assist in managing the risks between elements, although many contractors may have their own established methods of managing this risk.

3.4 Collaborative working

Earlier in this chapter we considered how co-ordination is **making** people or things work together for a common goal. Collaboration involves two or more people **working together** towards a common goal. In other words, it could be said that the efforts of the lead designer to co-ordinate the design may result in a co-ordinated design but that a co-ordinated design would be an inherent part of a collaborative process.

KEY TERM   **Collaboration** to work together, especially in a joint intellectual effort.

TABLE 3.1: Obstacles to collaborative working

OBSTACLE	SOLUTION
The remoteness of project designers	
Each designer on a project is typically based in their own practice's office. Collaborative tools such as extranets make it easier to transfer information; however, communication is predominately by e-mail or telephone conversation.	• Face-to-face workshops are critical to collaborative working and means of facilitating these are essential. • Locate the design team in a single base, allowing them to work together as a group in order to resolve issues as they arise. This might involve, for example, the M&E and C&S consultants co-locating their entire team in the lead consultant's office. • The lead consultant uses a co-ordinator who spends a substantial amount of time in the other designers' offices to ensure that co-ordination issues are dealt with timeously. • The M&E and C&S designers allocate co-ordinators who work between their own office and the architectural designer's office. • Web-based or video conferencing technology is used to allow better face-to-face communication between project meetings.
The way in which teams are assembled	
Teams are typically assembled in an ad hoc manner and, on many projects, practices and individuals are working together for the first time. This can create tensions as individuals need to get to know each other and procedural issues are inevitable as different internal processes come together for the first time.	• Research suggests that teams comprising individuals who have **all** worked together previously or those where **no one** has worked together are least effective. The most effective teams are a combination of practices and individuals who have worked together in the past with some new members. Form the team accordingly. • The lead consultant's involvement in the selection process of the other designers is essential. • The lead consultant selects, and appoints, the other designers as part of the bid process.
Appointment documentation	
Many bid documents suggest that clients want project teams to work collaboratively, but the appointment documents that they create for the project contain onerous and stringent clauses that make such an approach difficult.	• Use collaborative forms of appointment such as NEC3. • All of the designers agree to a charter while developing the project quality plan. This sets out the ways in which they will work collaboratively. • The deliverables to be produced by each designer at each stage are produced as well as the inputs required from other designers to achieve these. Any anomalies are discussed and agreed. • Determine the extent of specialist contractor design input at an early stage to allow the design to be produced accordingly.

CHAPTER 3 CO-ORDINATION, INTEGRATION AND COLLABORATION

OBSTACLE	SOLUTION
Software Different designers will use different software packages that are not compatible with each other. Models are kept on different servers, frequently resulting in some designers working on out-of-date background files.	• Some see 3D drafting and building integrated modelling (BIM) as being at the heart of the collaborative process and, while there is no doubt that this type of technology can assist the design process, there are other drivers that need to be considered. • Ensure that everyone's software is compatible. • If 3D software is being considered, examine how it will be used by all of the project designers. One designer failing to use the software will negate any benefits. • The use of 'clash detection' software is beneficial, but processes that avoid the clash in the first place are more effective.
Project processes If each designer works in their usual manner and delivers information 'as they have always done it', a team will fail. Statements such as 'we must do it that way to comply with our QA system' are, on the whole, smokescreens and barriers to collaborative working.	• Establish early workshops to agree the contents of the Project Quality Plan. These should cover deliverables, communication and all other aspects that will impact on the team's ability to work collaboratively. Align workshops to team-building events so that individuals who have not worked together can get to know each other. • Devise methods of efficiently and regularly transferring information, preferably electronically and preferably as 2D/3D drafting files. • Examine methods of working from a single server so that all parties are working on 'live' design files. • Consider what software will be used to mark-up 2D drawings or comment on 3D information.
Professional or cultural stances Individual consultants may have strong views on what their duties entail or what they will deliver and when. These preconceptions can make working relationships difficult, particularly when one designer requires information that another wants to provide at a later stage.	• The occasional stubbornness of designers in failing to provide the timely information required to develop the design can only be overcome by ensuring that companies and, more importantly, the individuals proposed for a project have open minds and are receptive to working in a collaborative manner. • Use initial team sessions to establish the Project Quality Plan, which should set out the deliverables for each designer at each stage and the processes that everyone will use to achieve them. • Develop a 'charter' setting out the measures that everyone will take to ensure that they work collaboratively and assist each other as the design develops.

From Table 3.1 it can be seen that there are a number of factors that make, or break, a great team. While it is true that a team has to want to work together collaboratively in order to do so, a number of obstacles to collaborative working must be considered.

In summary, 3D drafting can help a collaborative design process, but the most important aspect is the willingness of all members of the team to make the process work. The team must gel from the outset, establish how their procedures will dovetail and then meet face to face on a regular basis in order to quickly resolve ongoing co-ordination issues. It is essential that each designer understands the needs of the other designers in relation to the programme if each designer is to accomplish the goals of collaborative working.

Conclusion to Chapter 3
Co-ordination, Integration and Collaboration

ONE   It is essential that co-ordination takes place but it must be done progressively and the right tasks undertaken at the right time.

TWO   Once the design has been co-ordinated, contractor design work will still need to be integrated into this design work.

THREE   There may be benefits in subcontractors undertaking some of the design work. The scope of this should be agreed early in the project.

FOUR   Co-ordination is essential, but is more likely to occur when a team is working collaboratively.

CHAPTER 4
PROGRAMMING DESIGN

TIME IS INEVITABLY limited during every stage of a project and, with a multitude of design tasks to be undertaken and co-ordinated, programming is an essential component of good design management. As lead consultant and/or lead designer, you are likely to have obligations to co-ordinate the preparation of programmes; to successfully undertake these duties, programming must be taken seriously. In this chapter, we will highlight the aspects you need consider in order to produce succinct yet meaningful design programmes.

4.1 What programming duties do the lead consultant and lead designer have?

In the RIBA appointment document, the lead consultant and lead designer have obligations to produce programmes at each stage:

- the lead consultant is responsible for '*leading and co-ordinating ... work stage programmes; including work from the previous stage*'; and
- the lead designer is responsible for '*co-ordinating preparation of work stage programmes(s) for the design process*'.

What should the lead consultant's programme address in order to be successful?

One of the key functions of the lead consultant's programme is to set out known programme inputs, outputs or constraints and to compare these against the lead designer's programme. In order to produce his/her work stage programmes, the lead consultant must consider which parties will be contributing to that specific stage of the project and the timing of the various deliverables. Inputs might include:

LEADING THE TEAM

- feedback from precedent visits
- feedback from client user-groups
- feedback from client meetings
- feedback from stakeholders such as planners or amenity groups, and
- constraints dictated by statutory authorities (road access points, for example).

Examples of outputs would be:

- the completed stage report
- the cost plan
- a planning application
- the agreed brief.

Examples of constraints would be:

- client meeting dates
- one-off client meeting dates or special meetings
- planning meetings or meetings with other stakeholders
- dates by which information is required from utilities companies in order to progress the design
- approval periods (planning consent, for example)
- planning committee dates
- sign-off periods and processes
- CABE, or other statutory bodies', committee dates.

Elements of a stage report might also need to be considered early. For example, the estates committee may wish to agree to the access and cleaning strategy (see Tool 7 in Chapter 6) in advance of the final stage C or D report.

What should the lead designer's programme address in order to be successful?

Initially, the lead designer should be focusing solely on the design process and how it should be programmed and must consider how their programme will:

- deal with the iterative nature of design in the early stages;

- acknowledge that design proposals are presented to many people whose comments cannot be predicted;
- ensure adequate time for preparing options;
- ensure that user consultations do not 'drift' too far into the stage C programme duration;
- consider the different parties contributing to the design at different stages;
- allow for the input from specialist subcontractors who may have design responsibilities.

The lead designer's programme should also be based on previously established typical periods of time and processes for a project of a similar nature and scale, and, where possible, benchmarked against previous design programmes. Once the programme is completed in draft, any mismatch between the lead consultant's and lead designer's programmes can be identified and resolved.

Reconciling the lead consultant's and lead designer's programmes

Most changes to design programmes are driven by the dates that can be arranged for meetings or presentations. Some organisations may have to arrange meetings months in advance or meetings may have to be given to quarterly steering groups or other parties. In many situations the lead consultant and the designer are the same individual, or at least the same practice, and a single programme will be prepared. Whether it is a single programme or two programmes by two parties, the programme will need to be reconciled by:

- setting up meetings well in advance;
- ensuring that meetings are confirmed in writing and invitations sent to the relevant parties;
- programming 'follow-up' meetings (cancelling a meeting is easier than arranging a new date at short notice);
- considering how the design process is impacted by agreed dates;
- ensuring that all parties 'buy in' to the periods and milestones that are shown.

What are the risks to the designers?

Third party organisations present some of the biggest risks on a project: they are not employed by the client and therefore neither the client nor the design team can dictate programme terms to them. They are influenced by their own deadlines and pressures, which might dictate that other projects take precedence. They will include planners, statutory consultation groups and utility companies, among others.

The risks to the designers are that key decisions on plans or elevations, for example, those requested by the client or the planners, are made late in a stage, making co-ordination and finalising of the cost plan difficult. However, by considering potential issues at the start of a stage, means of managing them can be discussed and agreed with the client/project manager. In some instances, the team will require more time; in others it might be more appropriate to maintain the programme as long as the client has accepted the risks. Frequently, a hybrid solution might be agreed once an issue has been identified; for example, the client might accept that the cost plan is based on an earlier version of the elevations.

4.2 What is the master programme?

The master programme is typically produced by the project manager, and sets out the strategic dates that the client wishes to achieve from the commencement date to the day the project is handed over, along with other milestones the client might have. In preparing the master programme, certain stages may have been compressed or overlapped in order to achieve the required completion date or to comply with milestones (for example, a funding application).

If the construction period has been properly considered and benchmarked against previous projects it will be difficult to compress this period unless the design and construction can be overlapped and the resultant cost uncertainty can be accommodated. It is therefore likely that compression of a programme, for any reason, will impact on the work of the designers.

The designers, and in particular the lead designer, need to consider the implications that deviations from their standard programmes and working methods might have on the design process and the risks that may be encountered. These might include:

- design progressing to the next stage prior to the current stage being signed off by the client;
- planning consent being applied for earlier in the design process;
- planning applications running concurrently with stage E and/or F design;
- clients only being available on certain dates;
- insufficient time to co-ordinate the design;
- a specific designer's information being incomplete due to time constraints; or
- insufficient time to finalise the cost plan.

Many of the risks created by the master programme can be dealt with by the fine tuning of the lead consultant/designer's work stage programmes and methods of dealing with these risks are considered below.

At a strategic programming level the designers need to consider the risks of overlapping activities. For example, if the planning application is running in parallel with the progression of stage E/F information, is the client taking the cost risk for any redesign work resulting from conditions imposed on the planning consent? If not, perhaps the designers should not progress with their stage information. In any case, additional measures should be put in place to try to mitigate the risk which arises from such programming decisions.

4.3 The iterative design process

The iterative design process has achieved greater recognition in the manufacturing industries than it currently has in the construction industry. It involves a prototype being refined in an iterative manner until it is ready to be put into mass production, and is essential in preventing design or manufacturing errors that could have significant ramifications once a product has gone into mass production.

KEY TERM **Iteration** is the act of repeating a process with the aim of achieving a specific objective. Each repetition of the process is called an 'iteration', and the results of one iteration become the starting point for the next.

LEADING THE TEAM

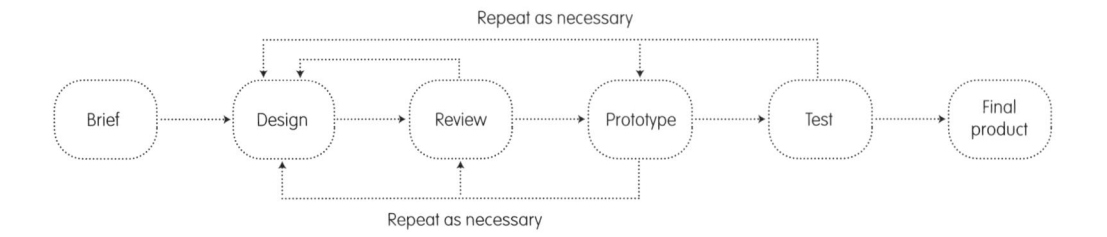

```
                         Repeat as necessary
        ┌─────────────────────────────────────────────────┐
        │                                                 │
  Brief ──→ Design ──→ Review ──→ Prototype ──→ Test ──→ Final
              ↑          ↑           │                   product
              │          │           │
              └──────────┴───────────┘
                  Repeat as necessary
```

FIGURE 4.1: Iterative design loop

KEY TERM   **Iterative design** is a **design** methodology undertaken using a cyclical process of **prototyping**, testing, analysing and refining a product or process. Based on the results of the most recent iteration, changes and refinements are made. This process is intended ultimately to improve the quality and functionality of the final design.

The iterative process on a building project cannot be implemented to the same stringent levels as with a product being developed for manufacturing because:

- timescales limit the number of iterations that can occur;
- many other designers and outputs are involved in the process; and
- each building is unique, due to the many factors that influence the design.

Is iteration possible in building design?

There are typically two periods of iterative design in a building project:

- during stages C, D and E when the GA drawings are being developed; and
- during stage F2 when the contribution of specialist subcontractors will require iteration of detailed aspects of the design. This is dealt with in the next section.

CHAPTER 4 PROGRAMMING DESIGN

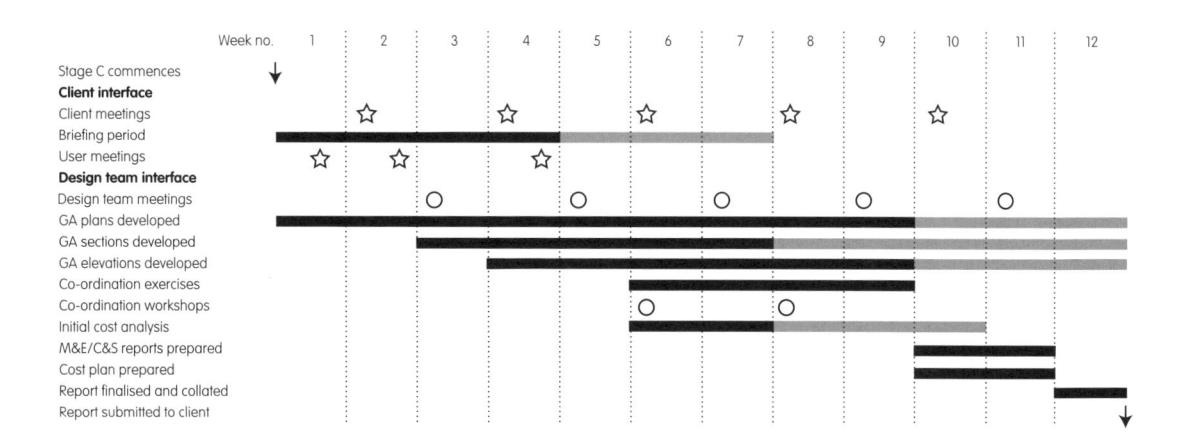

FIGURE 4.2: Stage C programme

The iterations of the GA drawings during stage C typically consist of amendments in response to:

- comments made at client presentations;
- comments made at user meetings;
- comments from third parties, such as planners;
- the analysis and conclusion on the most appropriate structural grids; and
- the development of M&E elements (i.e. plantroom and riser requirements).

To complicate matters further, the GA drawings will be developing while some or all of these iterations are occurring concurrently, and potentially impacting on each other. **Detailed** bar chart programmes, where one activity logically follows the other, serve no purpose as the iterative process may require a specific activity to be repeated.

> **Stated in another way: if the output of a specific programme bar cannot be predicted with certainty then it cannot be programmed as a finite item in a programme.**

The only way to overcome this is to set out activities in programmes on a very broad brush basis such as 'GA plans developed' or 'GA elevations developed' with these not shown as being finalised until the stage report is prepared and issued. Figure 4.2 illustrates how this would work. Chapter 3, in the section headed Co-ordination, set out how the M&E and C&S aspects should be kept at a strategic level at stage C, with neither designer producing GA information. This approach is also highlighted in Figure 4.2. The shaded durations are used to imply that certain activities may extend to the end of the stage.

Programming in this manner resolves the iterative design conundrum. More importantly, it makes it clear to the other designers that they have focused contributions to make at the right time and that they will have to develop their 'outline proposals for structural and building services systems' in parallel. The programme in Figure 4.2 makes this clear and, more importantly, makes it clear that the architectural designer requires time to take stock of various inputs at various times and is focused on getting the concept right. The programme also shows that the cost consultant is developing the cost plan before the final iteration of the design. This is covered further in Chapter 5: Managing cost.

However, by creating a 'looser' programme that is more representative of the iterative process, the lead designer needs to consider other tools that can be used in conjunction with the programme in order to manage the design process and to demonstrate that, in overall terms, the design is progressing on programme.

Other tools to use in conjunction with a design programme

Design status schedule

The design status schedule can perform a number of functions (covered further in Chapter 6: Eight essential design management tools) and serves different purposes at different stages of the design. Its primary functions are to act as a bridge between the information 'in the designer's head', the current design drawings and as a means of conveying all aspects of the developing design to each of the relevant parties.

Progress reports

It is essential that progress reports contain a commentary in relation to the programme and, in particular, to tasks that are behind programme or have not taken place (planned vs actual design progress). Key design team issues (hot topics) can be extracted from the design status schedule for discussion. Topics (discussed further in Chapter 6) to consider are:

- specialists, such as catering consultant, not being appointed;
- extensive comments from planners that are prolonging the development of the elevations;
- user group comments taking longer than anticipated to close out;
- new comments received from a separate internal client group;
- lack of detailed responses from utilities companies; and
- meetings being cancelled by third parties.

CHAPTER 4 PROGRAMMING DESIGN

An appropriate analogy of the iterative process would be a shepherd (lead consultant) and his dog (design status schedule) corralling sheep (design issues) across a field into a pen (stage report). The shepherd sees the overall direction of the sheep, the dog marshals rogue sheep and, eventually, they are all directed into the pen. The process of concluding a stage report is similar!

How should the design programme for stage D vary from the stage C programme?

The preparation of the stage D programme will use similar techniques to stage C and the starting point will be dealing with any outstanding stage C items. Once these have been determined and planned, a programme for the rest of the stage can be prepared. As the design will be 'settling down', the number of iterative items will be reduced and the durations for activities can be more specific. At stage D, the programme might therefore resemble that shown in Figure 4.3.

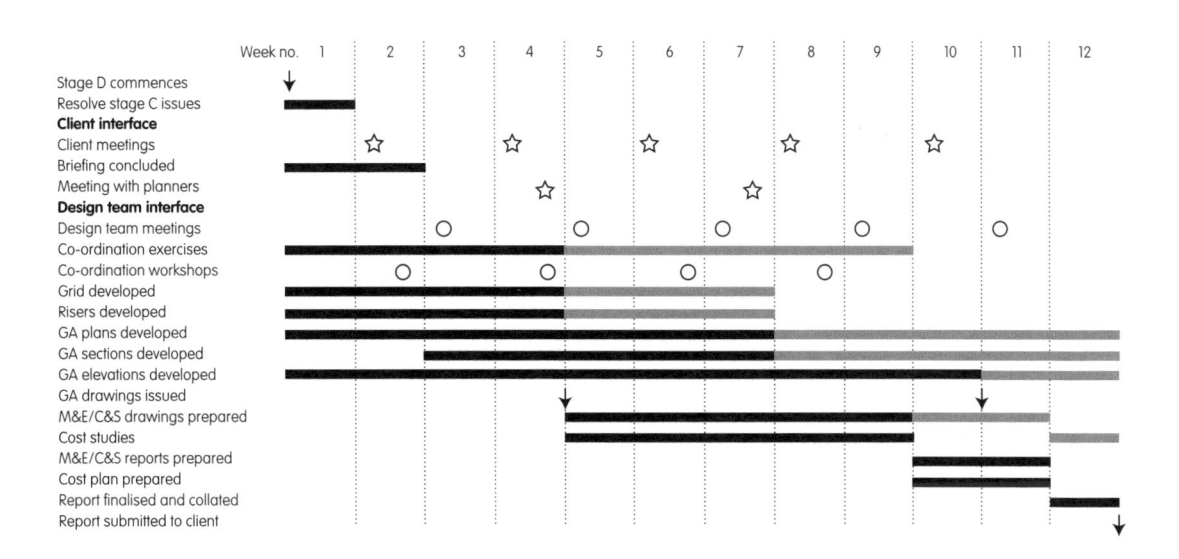

FIGURE 4.3: Stage D programme

45

What should the design programmes for stage E contain?

The 2007 Plan of Work (amended in November 2008) defines stage E as the *'Preparation of technical design(s) and specifications, sufficient to co-ordinate components and elements of the project and information for statutory standards and construction safety'*. Though this description is open to interpretation it can be stated that:

- if co-ordination of the design has been undertaken (as set out in Chapter 3), stage E should be dealing with residual co-ordination issues;
- at the end of stage E, the co-ordination of the design should be sufficiently complete to allow architectural, C&S and M&E production information to progress independently with the minimum of discussion between designers; and
- the GA drawings should be 'frozen' at the end of stage E. Amending them during stage F will result in programme delays or in the C&S and M&E tender information showing a different architectural layout.

With the major iterative elements of the design complete by the end of stage E, different drivers inform how the design information for the subsequent stages should be programmed.

If the design status schedule has been properly established and developed, it should be clear what tasks need to be concluded in order to 'freeze' the architectural GA drawings and, due to the short duration likely to be available and the fact that stage E might run concurrently with stage F, a specific work stage programme for this stage may not be necessary or justified. If a programme is produced it should be similar in format to the stage D programme.

What are the design programme issues at stage F1?

Stage F1 is the 'preparation of production information in sufficient detail to enable tenders to be received'. This information may be issued as a single entity or, depending on the method of procurement, as packages (see Chapter 3). Before stage F1 commences it is essential to agree:

- the extent of performance specified work; and
- how much information will be issued for tender.

Whether the programme is generous or compressed, a programme at stage F1 is useful and should set out when each element of the design will be prepared so that the tender issue date is achieved. This programme needs to take account of the work of the cost consultant, who may be preparing bills of quantities or pricing documents, and also needs to specify a period for collating the information before issue. In some instances, a pre-tender estimate may be requested by the client, although it is perhaps best that this is undertaken in parallel with the tendering process.

Such programmes will also assist the designers to determine resourcing requirements: the number of staff and the skill sets or knowledge required. In addition, any design dependencies can be identified and factored into the programme. This is covered further in the next section, but can include the ceiling layouts being produced and issued to the M&E designer to enable lights, grilles, smoke detectors or other services to be added.

Stage F may run concurrently with stage E and, where this takes place, it is advisable to ensure that any elements of work that are being progressed will not be affected by the outputs of stage E (finalised GA drawings).

How does a programme for stage F2 differ from stage F1?

Once a contractor has been appointed, the designers need to finalise their production information that was issued for tender, along with any additional information deemed necessary, and issue it for construction. On larger projects this information might be issued in tranches to allow the designers to maintain a consistent level of resource rather than significantly enlarging the project team for a short period of time.

KEY TERM **Lead-in period** this is the period that a subcontractor requires between the placing of an order and starting work on site. The period will include the time required for the production and review of any design information, the time required to procure materials and the manufacturing and delivery periods.

The lead consultant, in collaboration with the lead designer and other designers, should prepare a design programme for stage F2 and include it within the tender documents issued to the contractors. When the tenders are returned, they can assess this programme against the various contractors' construction programmes once they have allowed for the relevant lead-in periods. Any deviations can then be discussed, and agreed, during post-tender negotiations with contractors. By doing so, the design team has a greater chance of agreeing a more amenable programme, that is configured to their internal resource requirements and design activities.

If the designers do not produce a programme, it is possible that the contractor will prepare their own, perhaps in the form of a 'Deliverables List', that sets out dates when information is required. This is likely to be more onerous, and it is certainly more difficult for the lead designer to negotiate such dates when the contractor is appointed and has ownership of the schedule.

We have already demonstrated that a programme for stage F1 was not essential, but that it had a number of benefits. A programme at stage F2 **is** essential, as any delays in releasing construction information could result in a delay to construction activities on site. When considering this, it may be prudent to issue an internal programme for the release of information that is a week ahead of the agreed programme. So, if information is issued a few days 'late' it will, in reality, have been issued a few days early!

With specialist subcontractors designing during this period, any design dependencies become of even greater relevance. These are discussed in the next section.

While the GA drawings may not change, the detailed aspects of the design will not be finite and complete until all the specialists have completed their designs. Until this occurs, the residual design issues, or risks, will need to be programmed, monitored and managed until they have been closed out.

4.4 Design dependency
– don't forget about the other designers!

Design dependency is the single biggest item that needs to be understood by the lead designer for the successful co-ordination of the design and, where required, integration of the specialist contractors' design work into the project.

Design dependency is where the work of one designer cannot commence or be completed until the work of another designer has been provided (i.e. where one designer is dependent on the output from another designer in order to progress his/her own design). When both designers are specialist subcontractors, there can be a significant knock-on impact on the construction programme if the dependencies related to their work have not been properly thought through.

Examples of design dependency and how they might be overcome

- At stage C the architect cannot add plantrooms and main risers to the developing plans until a plantroom and riser schedule is received from the M&E designer defining these requirements. While the design status schedule may state when this information is required, there may be benefits in having a milestone date in a programme in order to monitor this item more closely. However, an iterative process may be required to enable the M&E designer to produce this schedule. (Are we using gas, electricity, renewable energy? Where do the utilities companies want incoming supplies to be located?) And, afterwards, there will certainly be an iterative process to determine a location and size to fit within the building concept and the emerging structural grids. Programming and persistent discussions at design workshops are the only means of driving these key co-ordination aspects to a conclusion.
- Without 'frozen' GA drawings, neither the C&S nor the M&S engineers can commence their own detail drawings. They are reliant on the architect's CAD files to use as background information. Changes to these for any reason, once they have commenced their design, will impact on the date on which they deliver their information or its accuracy and therefore the level of co-ordination that has been achieved. The section on co-ordination in Chapter 3 sets out how best to manage this issue.
- Without a ceiling grid layout, the M&E consultant cannot begin to position grilles, light fittings and any other services component located in the ceiling.

LEADING THE TEAM

> To overcome this, a ceiling layout should be developed early in the design process. Ideally, a layout will be issued at stage E, but the M&E principles will then need to be discussed at design workshops. The ceiling plan is a key co-ordination deliverable.
> - The location of curtain walling brackets, stair or atrium balustrading brackets and their method of fixing are required from the relevant subcontractor. They might be fixed from the top or side and these variables may impact on the design of the adjacent structure, which may already have been constructed. To overcome this, any constraints should therefore be stated on the design intent drawings, with the principles of fixing discussed with the structural engineer to enable load allowances to be made when designing the main frame.
> - An access system for cleaning facades is proposed on the roof. With every manufacturer having different rail details and support plinth centres, the structural engineering designer cannot issue construction information for the roof until this information is provided. The design intent information might be created to be flexible in this regard, allowing all of the systems to be compliant at tender stage and therefore allowing the most competitive price. However, if the procurement cycle stalls, and the subcontractor is brought on late and is therefore unable to complete the design, there could be delays to the structural engineer issuing the roof slab information, resulting in a claim from the concrete subcontractor. There is no specific solution to this, other than to press the contractor to obtain design information from the gantry manufacturer as early as possible and, more importantly, to highlight the need for this.

Managing design dependencies

Once dependencies have been identified, it becomes easier to manage them and the main challenge for the lead designer is to consider what these dependencies are. Once identified, there are a number of methods for managing them:

- Milestones can be included in the design programme for critical dependencies, such as the issue of plantroom schedules or CAD files of the ceiling layouts.
- The design status schedule can be used to add and track less critical, but nonetheless important, dependencies. And, as noted in Chapter 3, the design status schedule can also be used to track dependencies that impact on the earlier, more iterative stages of design.

- Activities can be reprogrammed and thereby produced earlier than originally anticipated by a designer, and this demonstrates the successful consideration of design dependency. This is of particular importance with the work of specialist subcontractors whose packages may have to be procured earlier in order to close out certain design dependencies.
- Structural work commences on site at the beginning of the construction period and many difficult design dependencies arise from architectural or M&E elements that interface with this work. The late resolution of these interfaces can have significant cost and time implications and, to overcome this, these design aspects need either to be designed with the main frame or in a manner that allows them to be detailed later in the construction process. For example, brackets for an external canopy can be detailed in the main frame with the canopy designed at a later date.
- The design team can make assumptions and then ensure that those tendering are aware of these (using the design status schedule) and the tenderers can then price on the basis of these assumptions. An example of this would be the lift size dimensions, as mentioned in Chapter 3 above.

In conclusion, every design dependency needs to be considered and, if the design programme cannot successfully be used to deal with the interface once activities have been reprogrammed, then other methods must be used. These might include the careful design of interfaces, or making assumptions that are converted into tender constraints. Overall, the design status schedule should be used to track such risks until they are closed out.

4.5 How does the contractor's construction programme differ from design programmes?

The construction programme, which is produced by the contractor, performs a number of crucial functions:

- It enables the contractor to demonstrate and be confident that the building can be constructed in the period allocated by the client in the tender. In some instances, the contractor may propose a shorter construction period to gain commercial advantage and to reduce preliminary costs.

- It allows construction progress on site to be monitored against planned progress.
- It acts as a framework for the subcontract programmes produced by the many subcontractors likely to be working on a project (these programmes may also be contractual in their nature).
- It identifies the critical path of the project (this is covered in more detail below).
- It provides others, such as the contract administrator on traditional contracts, with information required to assess extensions of time or other contractual issues.

A review of the construction programme by the lead consultant and lead designer is also useful as it:

- may identify a construction sequence that is not possible due to the way that a specific area is detailed;
- enables them to ensure that their proposed dates for the release of construction information, whether by element or building area, are in line with the construction programme; and
- allows them to understand the critical path activities: where delays in the release of design information may have a significant impact on programme.

A construction programme is prepared using 'frozen' information (typically the GA drawings) and, once the contractor's programmer has established the quantities of work for each element and area of the building, he/she can use personal knowledge, or historical data from completed projects, to prepare the programme. The contractor may generate different versions of the construction programme for different purposes. For example, the contract programme will never change and will be used for monitoring progress; however, a different programme might be used internally in an attempt to construct the building more quickly (thereby reducing the contractor's prelims) or in order to recover lost time where delays have occurred. Some of these points are covered below.

Planned vs actual progress

At monthly progress meetings the contractor's report typically sets out where the **actual** progress on site sits in relation to the **planned** progress. Earlier in this chapter we looked at how considering planned vs actual design progress allowed designers to set out how

CHAPTER 4 PROGRAMMING DESIGN

design aspects, which were not progressing in line with the programme, were being managed and/or the resulting delays mitigated. Similarly, the contractor should use his/her own analysis of planned vs actual construction progress to set out how construction delays are being managed and how any delays to the programme might be recovered.

What is the critical path?

The shortest possible duration for the completion of a project is determined by the critical path. An activity becomes a critical path activity if its late completion would result in the late completion of the entire project. Understanding the critical path is therefore essential, as delay to activities that are not on the critical path will not necessarily lead to a delay in the project completion.

To illustrate this, the programme in Figure 4.4 shows that the completion of the frame on each level allows the installation of blockwork to commence and that the completion of blockwork then allows the toilet fit-out elements to commence. The completion of all of the toilets signifies project completion. The toilet complexity is significantly larger

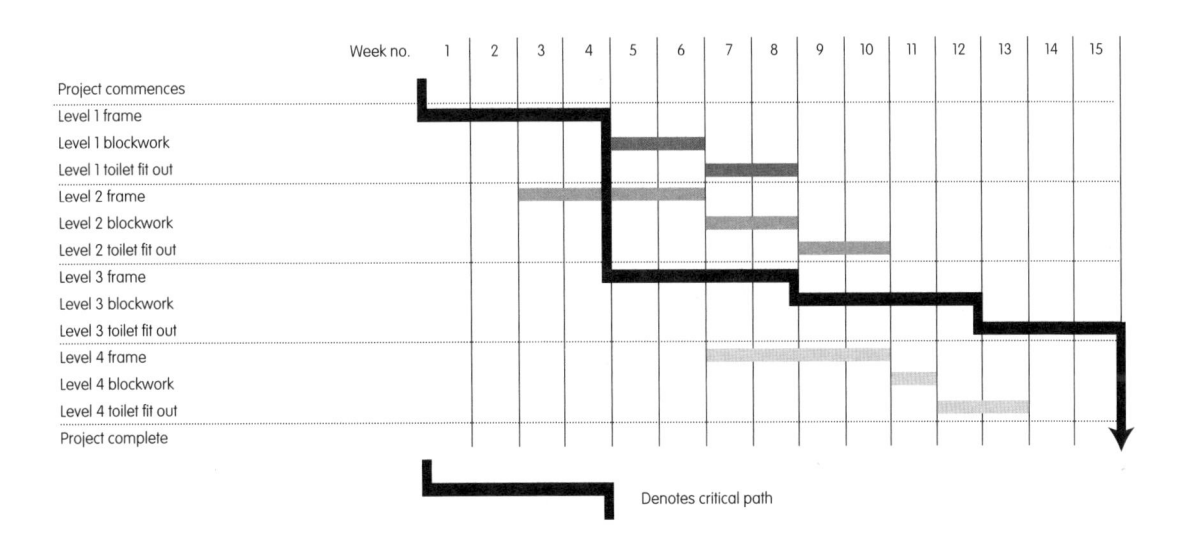

FIGURE 4.4: Critical path programme

on level 3 (perhaps the changing rooms of a gym), reflected in a longer construction duration, and it can be seen that a delay to this activity, and any preceding it, will delay the completion date. This therefore generates the critical path. Items that are not on the critical path will not immediately delay the overall completion if they are behind programme; however, if the delay becomes significant then this would clearly not be the case. Using the example of Figure 4.4, if the fourth floor toilets were delayed by more than two weeks, the activity would come onto the critical path and delay the project completion date. Of course, this is a simplified example and, in reality, there are significantly more activities on a project, making the critical path difficult to determine and understand.

Why is 'float' included in the programme?

It is prudent for any programme to contain a degree of float as it is almost inevitable that one or more aspects of a project will be delayed. Programmes issued externally by the contractor may not show such float as this would suggest that an earlier completion date is achievable, although it is likely that the contractor's internal version of the programme contains float or has an earlier completion date. With the contractor possibly having to pay penalties for late completion, such measures are understandable.

The lesson that the lead consultant or designer can take from this is that any design programme can benefit from a degree of float. For example, if the architectural team has a contractual commitment (which is likely on many contracts) to release a curtain walling package on a certain date, then it is prudent for any internal programme date to be earlier, perhaps by a week.

Conclusion to Chapter 4
Programming Design

ONE — The risks associated with strategic programmes need to be considered and means of managing the risks associated with compressed or out-of-sequence design work agreed.

TWO — Work stage programmes produced by the lead consultant must consider the various aspects that have to occur in order for the design to progress.

THREE — Design programmes must be produced and reviewed against the lead consultant's programme, with any amendments made and the methods of dealing with the resultant risks agreed.

FOUR — The iterative nature of design makes it difficult for the lead designer to produce a front-end design programme and he/she must consider other tools to be used in conjunction with the design programme.

FIVE — The later stages of the design are easier to programme, as the design becomes more fixed in its nature.

SIX — Designers need to understand the information that other designers 'depend on' (dependencies) when preparing their design programme.

CHAPTER 5
MANAGING COST

IN THIS CHAPTER, we consider the role of, and relationship with, the cost consultant. This is a crucial relationship for any designer as most clients consider the cost consultant as their 'banker' (taking care of their money) and the best designers need to demonstrate that they are treating the client's money as they would their own. Besides, you may produce your best-ever design, but if that significantly exceeds the client's budget, it will never progress. Designing to budget is therefore a core design skill and, in this chapter, this skill and how to interface with the cost consultant are considered.

The cost consultant has a different role to the other consultants: they are seen as being 'closer' to the client, as all clients value their money and want to ensure that the project is completed on budget. While it is increasingly common for the lead consultant to appoint the C&S and M&E designers as subconsultants, it is unusual for the lead consultant to be asked to appoint the cost consultant. This underlines how clients like to maintain a direct relationship with their cost consultant.

5.1 What are the duties of the various consultants in relation to cost?

In the RIBA appointment, the duties of each role in relation to cost are as detailed below.

- Lead consultant:
    - 'monitoring the work of the consultants';
    - 'developing and managing change control procedures, and making or obtaining decisions necessary for time and cost control';
    - 'receiving regular status reports from each consultant'; and
    - 'issuing instructions reasonably necessary for the purpose of time and cost control or co-ordination of design work within the scope of the Project subject to obtaining prior approval of the client'.

- Designers (including lead designer):
    - 'providing design specifications, advice and information concerning the design for which the designer is responsible ('the Relevant Design') with due regard to cost, functionality, build quality and impact, buildability, construction safety, operation and maintenance'.
- Cost consultant:
    - 'providing estimates, advice, valuations and other information concerning the cost of construction works'; and
    - 'co-ordinating and integrating estimates, advice, valuations and information provided by any other person'.

Part 2: Design Services of the schedules element of the RIBA appointment document clarifies further what the architect is required to do at each stage of the project but, more importantly, these statements succinctly set out what the status of the estimate of the construction cost (cost plan) will be.

STAGE C	'Providing information for approximate estimate of the Construction Cost'
STAGE D	'Providing information for estimate of the Construction Cost'
STAGE E	'Providing information for updating estimate of the Construction Cost'
STAGE F1	'Providing information for updating estimate of the Construction Cost'
STAGE G	'Providing information for preparation of pre-tender estimate of the Construction Cost'

What can be concluded from this review of duties?

From a review of the above duties, the following role and responsibilities can be summarised:

- The designers provide the cost consultant with sufficient information to enable an estimate of the construction cost to be provided at each stage.
- The cost consultant must take into account cost information provided by others when producing the estimate.
- The lead consultant is required to monitor the work of the cost consultant and receive regular reports from him/her.

- The lead consultant is required to establish and maintain a change control procedure.
- The construction cost estimate at stage C will be approximate and, following its issue at stage D, it will be updated at stages E and F1 and at stage G it becomes a pre-tender estimate.

Are there any risks that the RIBA appointment does not address?

The RIBA appointment clarifies that the target cost is replaced by the first professionally prepared estimate approved by the client. What is not usually clear in the appointment documents is what occurs when the contractor's tenders are returned over budget or, earlier in the design process, if the stage D cost plan is over budget.

Before we consider what steps the designers, and in particular the lead designer, might take to ensure that the cost plan is accurate, thereby negating the need to redesign, we will briefly consider why a cost plan might be over budget.

5.2 The cost plan

The client's target cost for constructing the project will be included in the architect's appointment, along with the client's initial statement of requirements and the project timetable. This target cost will typically have been produced by the cost consultant, but may have been produced by the client or the project manager using historical data or experience.

The target cost will be superseded by the '*first professionally prepared estimate approved by the client*'. This is typically referred to as the 'cost plan' and is produced by the cost consultant.

When the cost consultant produces the first version of the cost plan, at a stage when no specific design information may exist, they may use historical data drawn from similar building types, along with initial estimates for any site-specific abnormals which may have already been identified.

RIBA stages

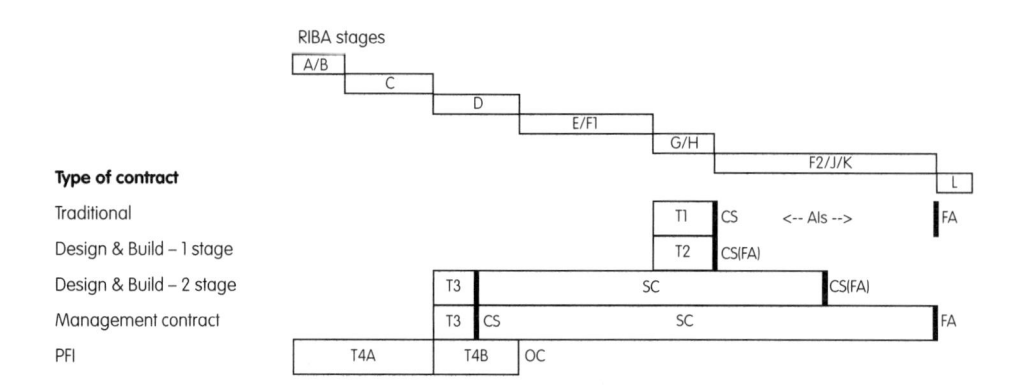

	A/B	C	D	E/F1	G/H	F2/J/K	L

Type of contract

Traditional						T1 │ CS <-- AIs --> │ FA
Design & Build – 1 stage						T2 │ CS(FA)
Design & Build – 2 stage			T3 │ SC │ CS(FA)
Management contract			T3 │ CS │ SC │ FA
PFI		T4A │ T4B │ OC

Key
T1 = Tendering with completed drawings and specifications (with bills of quantities or pricing schedule)
T2 = Employer's requirements (amount of F1 information will be less than traditional contract)
T3 = Tendering on profit, overheads and prelims only
T4A & B = Bid stages
SC = Subcontractor costs
CS = Contract sum
OC = Operational change
FA = Final account
AIs = Issue of architect's instructions

FIGURE 5.1: When do costs become fixed?

As the cost plan at stage C will be approximate, the allowance of a higher level of contingency within the cost plan can be justified. The stage D cost plan is the first proper estimate of the construction cost that is updated at stage E and stage F1, and possibly updated at the end of stage G after tenders have been issued. The latter estimate is also called a pre-tender estimate and may highlight the need for the designers to consider a list of savings before the tenders return.

When tenders are received, they should be similar to the cost plan, although many factors dictate that this is not always the case. Ultimately, the cost plan is superseded by the contractor's tender cost for constructing the project, which is quickly superseded by the agreed contract sum (which may be fixed or remeasurable).

Figure 5.1 illustrates that the timing of the shift from the cost plan amount, to the contractor's tender price to the contractor's final account varies depending on the form of contract and that, in some instances (management contracting, for example), the cost plan and contractor's costs will develop in parallel.

5.3 Why might the cost plan be over budget at a specific stage?

Earlier in the design process the cost consultant has to:

- consider any abnormal aspects (such as poor ground conditions);
- make assumptions on many items, including the level of specification;
- interpret the designers' drawings (making further assumptions); and
- use experience of market rates for carrying out elements of the work.

And, the cost consultant may not measure every aspect of the project in the initial stages, making further assumptions based on the brief, historical data or discussions with the design team.

If any of these assumptions are inaccurate, it is possible that the cost at the next stage will be over budget. The lead consultant and lead designer therefore need to consider how they can assist the cost consultant in ensuring that the estimate is accurate and means of doing this are set out below. In any case, two **significant** design management points need to be considered:

- The cost plan is typically produced at the **end** of a stage. However, if the cost exceeds the client's design budget, work will need to be undertaken to amend the design so that it is in line with the budget. Therefore, the development of the cost plan is a fundamental part of the iterative process and it is essential that measures are taken as the design progresses to ensure that the cost plan produced at the end of a stage reflects a design that is on budget.
- Many bespoke appointments will create an onerous onus on the designers to redesign at no extra cost should the cost plan be exceeded or the contractor's tenders be returned over budget. While the cost consultant will have a duty to ensure that his/her estimate is accurate, if the designers will not be paid to redesign work they should consider the interface with the cost consultant more closely and perhaps insist on specific duties, or processes or procedures that they require to ensure that the budget is not exceeded, being included in the cost consultant's scope of services.

LEADING THE TEAM

5.4 Getting the cost plan right
– what can the lead consultant/designer do?

There are a number of measures that the lead designer can consider to help ensure that the cost plan is as accurate as possible. The majority of measures (some of which are outlined below) are aimed at ensuring that the cost consultant is making the correct assumptions.

Sector and precedent information

Historical data is available industry-wide and cost consultants will also have access to historical data from previous projects to provide benchmarks. This will range from the cost per square metre for a specific building type to the cost per square metre rate for a specific element of the building. This data is adjusted by the cost consultant to take account of site abnormals (see below), regional issues (for example, costs tend to be higher in London) and market trends (are tender prices rising or falling?).

Architects, and other designers, can also obtain similar information from building studies that are published in magazines. This information can be a valuable design tool as it informs them where money is typically spent and what level of specification generally applies for items such as doors and toilets. The information can also be useful in allowing the lead designer to understand the level of M&E specification that occurs on a similar type of project.

Visits to project precedents can be useful in conveying aspects of a sector to a client and can also help initial discussions regarding finishes and fittings so that the client, designers and cost consultant all understand and agree the appropriate level of specification.

Elemental cost plan

The stage C cost plan is approximate and, as well as ensuring that there is a higher level of contingency at this stage, the lead designer should ensure that the cost plan is not simply based on industry-wide square metre rates. For example, the cost consultant might have taken the gross area and applied a rate for partitions to this figure. This will clearly be less accurate than if the cost consultant had measured the partitions shown on the drawings.

If the designers have duties to redesign if the project is over budget, they should agree when aspects of the design should be measured elementally. Just as co-ordination needs to occur incrementally, it may be that critical items, such as the elevations, are measured elementally at stage C with the interior aspects being considered at stage D.

Net vs gross areas

Historical data from other projects will typically be based on the gross area of a project. If the net to gross ratio of these projects can be understood, the lead designer will have a useful benchmark to use. For example, if the circulation area in a certain design is 25 per cent of the total area and, typically, projects in the sector have circulation areas of 20 per cent, then this design will be over budget unless the level of specification is reduced and this is agreed with the client. Otherwise, the plan will have to be made more efficient.

External wall area

While the net to gross figure is a good indicator of the efficiency of a plan, the amount of external wall can have a significant bearing on the cost plan, as a high proportion of building costs typically relate to the external envelope. For example, a square building has the most efficient external wall area in relation to the plan area, and atrium spaces, where external wall can be specified as internal walls, also help to reduce the amount of external walling. The architect therefore has to consider how this ratio and the level of specification being proposed for external materials will impact on the cost of the external wall, and it is prudent to produce draft elevations that can be measured as early as possible as part of the iterative process.

Mechanical and electrical (M&E) design

The M&E design contributes to a significant proportion of the building cost and, if the M&E designer has designed items that are not typically specified in a given sector, such as

- a complex lighting control system rather than a simple system (i.e. light switches);

- sophisticated control systems; or
- centralised vs localised water heating,

this may have a significant impact on the cost plan.

The lead designer must therefore ensure that when he/she is undertaking strategic co-ordination exercises, the level of specification being developed by the M&E designer is in line with sector norms.

Unique elements of design

If there are elements of the design that are innovative or unique, it is sensible for early discussions to be held with the subcontractors who might undertake such work. While the suppliers might be present, discussions with installers allow health and safety, buildability, prelims and other aspects to be properly addressed. Such discussions are frequently referred to as 'market testing' and allow the design to be fine-tuned in line with the specific design requirements of the specialist and enable the cost consultant to gain more accurate costing information on the specific design solutions that are being considered.

Level of specification/supplementary cost information

The timing for providing specification information to the cost consultant is crucial, as this can impact significantly on individual elements. Too much information too early would be counterproductive. In the next chapter the use of the design status schedule, to record discussions on each element of the design as the design progresses, is proposed. This can ensure that appropriate allowances are made for the proposed level of specification and for the unique aspects of a project. The schedule might, for example, record:

- deep reveals or projections requiring a larger flashing or other design feature that might not be immediately obvious on the GA elevations;
- the level of specification for different elements (for example, are the doors steel or timber? Do they require doorsets? If they are timber, what is the finish? Paint grade or laminate? Are they standard heights and widths?);
- the percentages of different ceiling finishes if a design has not been developed. For example, allowing for 30 per cent plasterboard (50 per cent of that having an acoustic specification) and 70 per cent 300 × 1000 mm metal tiles.

Cost consultants are certainly not mind-readers and the more focused information that can be gathered for each stage, the more accurate the cost plan will be.

Reviewing and monitoring the cost plan

Assuming the plan is efficient and that cost exercises have already been undertaken in relation to the external wall, it is essential that each version of the cost plan is issued to the designers in **draft** form to allow it to be reviewed before it is issued to a client. This allows the lead designer to be satisfied that the correct assumptions have been made on various items and enables either the design or the cost plan to be adjusted if necessary. To underline the importance of this draft issue, the date for its issue should be included in the stage programme with a period of time for review by the designers, and for the cost consultant to amend it, also shown.

Some cost consultants will issue the cost plan to the client **before** they issue it to the designers. This can be disruptive to the design process and the cost consultant should understand that the cost plan is part of the iterative design process and that designers must be given the opportunity to design to cost.

Cost exercises on specific items, such as the elevations, should also be built into the programme and scheduled for completion weeks in advance of the cost plan being finalised for a stage, as part of the process of ensuring that the design and cost are in harmony.

Furthermore, certain architectural practices may have specific materials, manufacturers or supplies, standard details or construction methodologies that they use and might have better historical cost data than the cost consultant, particularly where the practice has undertaken a number of buildings in the same sector using different cost consultants.

Most important of all, everyone should remember that design is an iterative process and that the establishment and adjustment of the cost plan are part of that process.

How should designers pass information to the cost consultant?

In Chapter 6, it is noted that the number of people attending design workshops must be limited if they are to be constructive. The cost consultant may not therefore be asked to attend every workshop, but the lead designer should certainly invite him/her if, while preparing for the workshop, the lead designer believes that cost may be a driver in the aspects that are being discussed.

While measurement of drawings will be the primary tool that the cost consultant uses to prepare the cost plan, this cannot work in isolation and it is essential that the designers meet with the cost consultant to discuss some of the subtle nuances that may exist in the design to ensure that allowances are made for these. The use of a design status schedule to record such meetings has already been discussed. Such meetings might also determine the assumptions that the cost consultant has made to date. There is no point in the designers considering oversized timber veneered doors with fire-rated glass panels and full-height offset stainless steel handles if the cost plan allows for paint grade doors with standard ironmongery.

What happens if the cost plan is over budget?

If the lead designer has ensured that the above measures have been put in place, each iteration of the design and the corresponding cost plan should align with the client's budget.

If this is not the case, it must be remembered that when a design has been produced, savings can only be made by making the building smaller (larger savings) or reducing specification (smaller savings). Each designer might rehearse what aspects of their design might create savings, particularly if the designer has a duty to redesign in the event of cost over-runs.

5.5 Why are whole life costs significant?

The construction cost of a project represents only a fraction of the costs associated with the life of a building (see Figure 5.2) and, because of this, clients are becoming more aware of life cycle costs and the impact that the maintenance strategy has on the whole

Design

Construction

Operation

Total cost of building

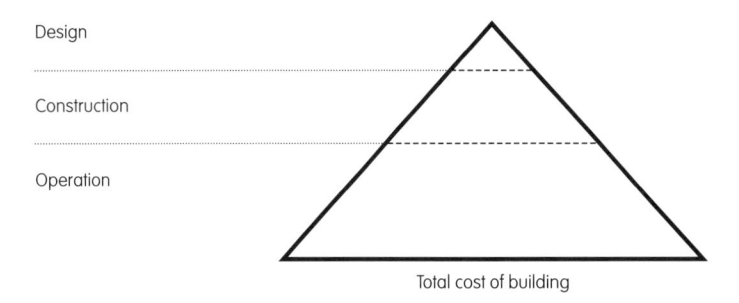

FIGURE 5.2: Whole life costs

life costs of a building. This is particularly the case where the client will also be the user and where the client's facilities management (FM) team is part of the design process.

Sustainability objectives also drive considerations: a building that has a considered maintenance strategy inevitably using less energy.

In Chapter 6 the benefits of preparing an initial cleaning and maintenance strategy at stage C, and the updating of this at stage D, are discussed along with the additional benefits of achieving health and safety objectives. Many life cycle considerations relate to the M&E systems of a building and it is important that the lead designer is aware of how the various M&E systems will be maintained in order to allow a holistic strategy for a building to be co-ordinated (for example, how plant on the roof will be replaced).

On PFI procurement routes, where the facilities management (FM) contractor is likely to be part of the bid consortium, FM costs constitute a substantial component of the overall bid cost and a more rigorous assessment of life cycle costs is essential; for example:

- different floor finishes with different life spans and cleaning regimes might be considered;
- more robust paint specification might be considered for corridors; and
- protection to corners in heavily trafficked areas might be specified.

Whether the high-level cleaning and maintenance strategy or more detailed aspects of a project are being considered, by reviewing these requirements early in the design process the lead designer can ensure that the requirements are embedded into the design, avoiding redesign and cost over-runs at a later stage and, by properly considering these elements, he/she will, by default, have provided a design with good life cycle credentials, a design that is safe to construct and maintain and one that is also environmentally sound.

5.6 Change control

KEY TERM **Change control** at stages C and D the design becomes aligned to a cost plan. Following the tender process, the tender design is then aligned to the contractor's cost for undertaking the work defined in the tender drawings. **Any** design changes following the sign-off of a stage report or a tender return have cost implications. These costs may be minor or significant (and in some instances savings may be made) and it is good practice to use a change control regime to involve the client in the change process and to ensure that the client's agreement to the design change(s) and the resultant cost implications is properly recorded.

Successful change control is fundamental to the financial management of a project. The RIBA appointment suggests that change is managed by the lead consultant, who is best placed to co-ordinate the impact of proposed changes with the client, designers and cost consultant. A well-managed change control system will ensure that change is properly considered and instructed **before** it is implemented, and will also ensure that designers are recompensed for amending their designs where this is appropriate.

It is essential that a change control process is agreed at the start of a project and included in the project quality plan. It should then be implemented at the appropriate stage of a project with the agreed processes properly managed and adhered to. The latest time at which change control should commence is at the end of stage D; however, introducing change control procedures at the commencement of stage D allows any procedures to be integrated into the design process and helps to drive home the point that change results in additional design costs as well as amendments to the cost plan sum.

When a project reaches site, change control should continue regardless of the form of procurement and it is essential that, if a traditional form of procurement is used, Architect's Instructions (AIs) are aligned with the change control regime and that they are not used to instruct change without the agreement of the client.

As the design progresses, change becomes more difficult to implement as more design work (depending on the complexity of the change) needs to be amended and this is

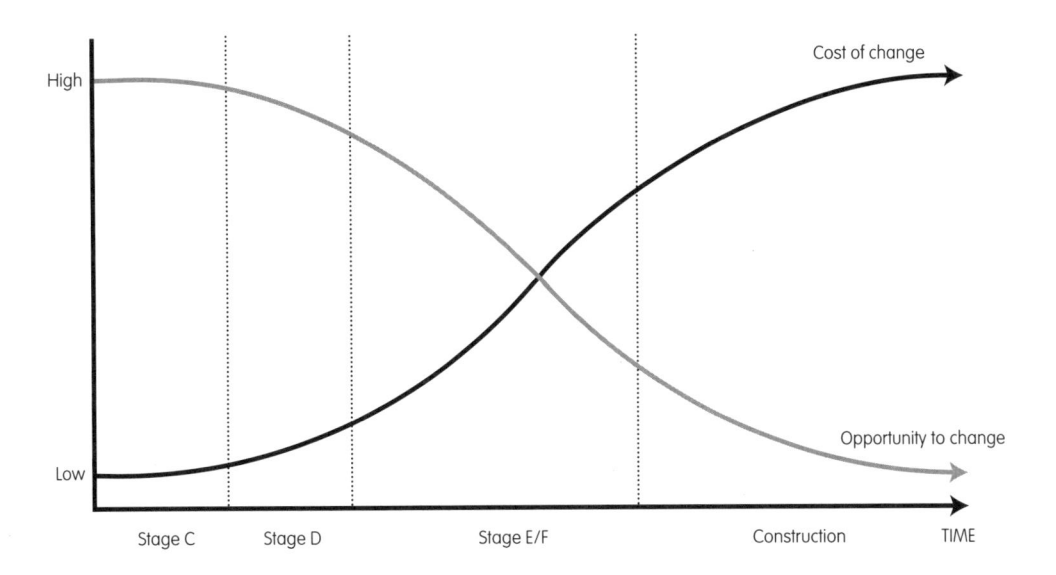

FIGURE 5.3: The cost of change

illustrated in Figure 5.3. Once a project commences on site, the costs and complexity of change increase further as elements may have been ordered, delivered and/or construction may have commenced on site.

What aspects should a change control form consider?

The contents of a change control form should be straightforward and it should, typically, include:

- the date the change request was raised;
- the nature of the change;
- the implications to the current design;
- the programme implications (design and construction); and
- the cost implications (design and construction).

A log should also be created to allow each change to be monitored and discussed at monthly progress meetings.

Are there any additional cost considerations once a project commences on site?

Time can be critical, particularly if a project is on site, and the cost of a given change may alter by the day if construction is ongoing around the area of proposed change. In this regard, the following cultural aspects need to be considered:

- How will design information be produced to enable the change to be costed? (Sketches may be quicker than CAD information.) If the work of a number of designers is impacted, how will this be co-ordinated?
- Designers should not underestimate the design costs of a change, particularly when the change has occurred after all design information has been issued for construction. They should not progress unless design costs are agreed or they are instructed to proceed on an hourly basis.
- No one should 'jump the gun'. Drawings and specifications should not be amended until the change is instructed by the client, who may not wish the change to progress once the cost implications have been clarified. In some situations, a separate team might be required to produce change information, with the 'construction' team only alerted to change when the client has instructed the change to proceed. This is common in the retail sector, where tenant changes can be significant.

5.7 What is value management and how does it differ from value engineering?

Value management (VM) fundamentally relates to the briefing process and, if correctly executed, can help to ensure, particularly on public-sector projects, that each space requested in the brief is a fundamental requirement and is adding value to the project. For example, different user groups may determine their own needs and a VM exercise might dictate that certain aspects (for example, staff rest rooms) are best shared between departments or collected into a single space.

Value engineering (VE) is a subset of value management and, if it is undertaken and facilitated properly, a VE workshop might question aspects of a concept, such as the use of an atrium or a particular M&E approach. VE exercises can ensure that each aspect of the design is robustly tested and adding value to the building.

When tenders are returned, cost exercises may be required to get the building back on budget and these may be a mixture of design team specification changes (such as reducing the lighting control system, amending the lift interiors, altering the proportion of materials on the elevation, or changing a specific finish) that can be costed by the contractor, or items that the contractor or specialist subcontractors might propose which can perhaps be more accurately defined as value engineering.

In some instances, the term VE is used where the cost plan is over budget and savings have to be considered. If the specification of certain items has to be **reduced** to resolve any budgetary issues or the area of the building reduced to resolve cost issues, then the term is arguably not appropriate. However, if the same design and specification are achieved by using a different design approach or methodology which may have been suggested by one of the design contractors, then this is true value engineering – achieving the same for less.

Conclusion to Chapter 5
Managing Cost

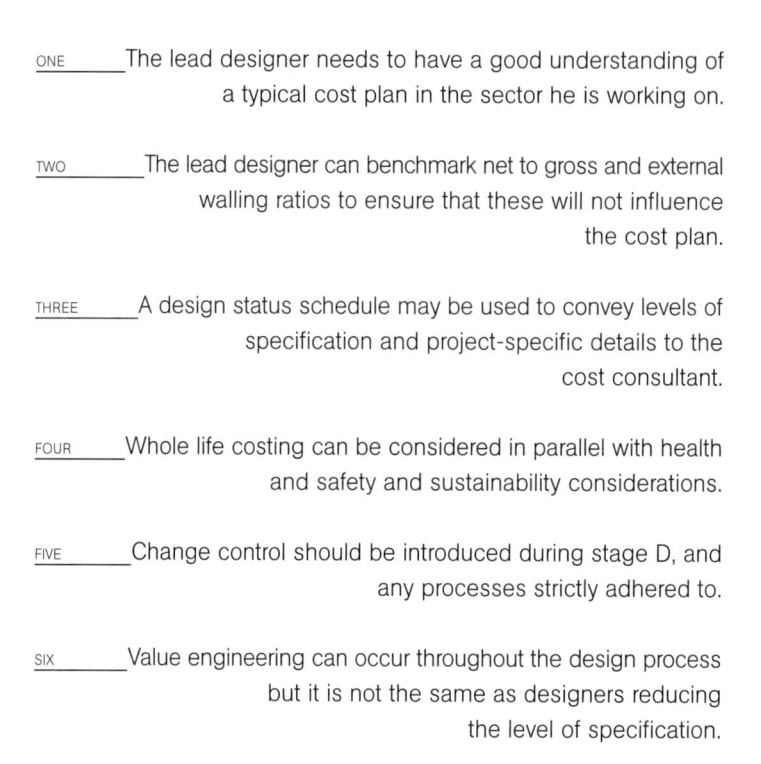

ONE — The lead designer needs to have a good understanding of a typical cost plan in the sector he is working on.

TWO — The lead designer can benchmark net to gross and external walling ratios to ensure that these will not influence the cost plan.

THREE — A design status schedule may be used to convey levels of specification and project-specific details to the cost consultant.

FOUR — Whole life costing can be considered in parallel with health and safety and sustainability considerations.

FIVE — Change control should be introduced during stage D, and any processes strictly adhered to.

SIX — Value engineering can occur throughout the design process but it is not the same as designers reducing the level of specification.

CHAPTER 6
EIGHT ESSENTIAL DESIGN MANAGEMENT TOOLS

IN THE INTRODUCTION, we saw how essential it is that knowledge about a project does not simply reside in the head of the lead consultant or lead designer, but that it is 'downloaded', shared and made available to everyone in the team. If this knowledge can be harnessed and made available to all, it can serve as a design tool, stimulate effective actions and responses among the team, facilitate planning and be used as a means of conveying the status of the design to the client.

There are numerous tools that can be employed to achieve this; however, no one tool will make the process successful. In reality, every tool has to be used. The secret of good design management is using the right tools at the right time and, to do this, the value that each tool brings to the design process must be understood. And, if a tool is not adding value at a specific point in time, it should not be used.

In this chapter we consider eight essential design management tools and gauge the value that each brings to the design process. Of course, the starting point of any design follows the appointment of the design team and the project quality plan acts as a useful tool for commencing the design management process.

TOOL 1: THE PROJECT QUALITY PLAN

On many projects, practices and/or the individuals from these practices will be working together for the first time. Different people work in different ways and practices have varying procedures or established cultural ways of working that teams are expected to follow. It is therefore essential at the start of a project to consider all aspects of communication, and any project procedures that will be adhered to, as well as agreeing the initial work stage programme.

The lead consultant is generally tasked with 'leading and co-ordinating the preparation of a project quality plan'. As it is likely that the culture established in initial meetings will prevail for the duration of a project, it is essential that a meeting is arranged at the commencement of a project to discuss the project quality plan, where ways of working can be discussed, agreed and recorded. It is also a crucial step in allowing the project design team to get to know each other better and, even when a team has worked together before, the meeting can still be useful for dealing with the issues specific to a new project.

What would a project quality plan include?

As well as recording agreements on items discussed at the 'start-up' meeting, such as communication or the issue of information, the project quality plan can serve a number of purposes. It should **not** be considered a static document and it should be updated on a regular basis as new parties become involved in a project and to take account of the development of the design, agreement of the procurement route and following the appointment of the contractor. Time spent preparing and updating the plan assists the effective running of a project. The plan might include:

- a team structure diagram to help to clarify contractual lines of responsibility;
- details of the practices involved in the project;
- the names and contact details of key contacts in each organisation;
- the strategic programme and work stage programmes as they are produced;
- agreed building zones, once the scale of outputs is increased (1:200 to 1:100, 1:50 or 1:20);
- the roles and responsibilities of each consultant;
- the agreed extent of contractor design;
- details on how information will be issued;
- agreed change control procedures and how these will operate; and
- the procedure for undertaking feedback at the end of the project.

Meetings to update the document regularly can also be used to:

- iron out any discrepancies in appointment documents;
- agree milestone dates, client review periods and discuss and agree other strategic design programme issues;
- brief new team members on the working methods being used on a project;
- fine tune verification processes as the project progresses;
- ensure that all the necessary consultants have been appointed; and
- formally record amendments to a practice's quality assurance procedures.

Some of these items are procedural or straightforward. However, the act of collecting them into a single document places a greater obligation on each consultant to ensure that their internal teams are briefed on how the project will run. Three items are worth a specific mention.

1 **Means of communication and transfer of information**
   The number and frequency of meetings, the use of e-mail, telephone or other means of verbal communication and the method of transferring information (e-mail, extranet, FTP site, file zipping) are varied. Project-specific agreements make design management more efficient.

2 **Change control strategy**
   Chapter 5 covers change control in detail but it is worth noting here that by setting out when change control will commence, and how it will be operated, early in the process there is a greater likelihood that the system will operate more effectively when it commences.

3 **Measuring achievement**
   Chapter 9 discusses the subject of continual improvement further. The project quality plan should set out when reviews will take place and the agenda for these reviews. There would certainly be a review at the end of a project (see post-occupancy evaluation in Chapter 9), but reviews at intermediate gateway stages can also perform a useful function.

A comprehensive and agreed project quality plan allows everyone to work more efficiently by eliminating any ambiguities, establishing effective means of communication and ensuring that everyone is working towards the same goals. More importantly, the initial steps taken to produce the first version of the manual are a fundamental part of developing a collaborative team.

TOOL 2: BRIEFING TRACKER

The client's brief is the starting point on the majority of projects. Sometimes, the project team will be asked to test the brief on a number of potential sites. On other occasions, the brief might need to be adjusted to suit proposals derived from a stringent analysis of the site.

The brief itself might be a simple statement such as 'provide me with 8,000 square metres of office space' or 'we would like a two-bedroomed house with a large open-plan living and dining area'. Or, it might be a substantial document where room data sheets set out the precise requirements for every space required on the project. Regardless, it is likely that changes to the brief will be required to suit the specific nature of the design as the written brief transforms into a developing design. It is also likely that the brief will contain ambiguities or contradictions that need to be clarified and that additional information will be required.

Successful management of the briefing process is therefore an essential ingredient of an effective project. Conversely, a poorly managed briefing process can lead to ambiguities arising during the production stages of a project, requiring many drawings to be amended.

To manage the briefing process, it is suggested that a briefing tracker is established. This tracker can serve a number of purposes:

- record all agreed deviations from the initial brief;
- monitor areas of ambiguity where further clarification is required;
- set out derogations from the brief, and agreement to them;
- record agreements made in meetings or workshops;
- collect additional briefing queries and their responses; and
- record any other clarifications that are made.

By having a single document that records any discussions, correspondence or agreements in relation to the brief, or sets out additional information requirements and when they were confirmed, the history of the brief's development will be efficiently managed and the document can be an essential reference tool in the future when the reasoning behind certain decisions may not be clear and the need to back track on the decision-making process is required.

The document does not need to be complex and might only contain:

- the date an item is raised or changed;
- the relevant briefing section and the proposed change; and
- the status of the change (drawings to be amended, agreed by X on Y date).

In some instances, the document may become contractual, particularly on a D&B project where it might constitute part of the employer's requirements or be submitted with the contractor's proposals where it essential that any derogations from the brief are clear and agreed as part of the tender process. Or, it might become an appendix to the stage C and/or D reports. Where it does have a contractual nature, it will be essential for the lead consultant to ensure that the tracker takes precedence over the brief and that its status is properly recognised in any contractual documentation.

What other tools can be used to manage the briefing process?

In addition to utilising the briefing tracker, the lead consultant should ensure that all aspects of the briefing process and any user consultation periods are contained in the design programme and reviewed on a regular basis. The lead consultant and lead designer need to liaise and consider how much time will be required to deal with each stage of the briefing process, and to set out an overlay of all the key consultations on the design process. This is covered in greater detail in Chapter 4: Programming design.

TOOL 3: PROJECT MEETINGS

A good meeting structure is the backbone of a successful project. Different types of meetings will be required with each having a specific purpose. If design workshops are to be successful, they need to be set up and run in a different way to design team meetings and these differences are now considered.

How should design team meetings be set up and run?

The design team meeting (frequently called the monthly progress meeting) should primarily be a reporting meeting, where each designer reports on the progress of their design work. The project quality plan should set out the agenda and reporting formats, which should be aligned. The lead consultant may have an obligation to receive reports from each consultant in advance (the ideal contents are detailed in Tool 4), and ensuring that each consultant's report uses the same format allows the meeting to be run more effectively.

The key objective of the meeting should be to discuss how the design issues that have been identified in the individual reports will be resolved rather than undertaking the actual resolution (although in certain circumstances this may be appropriate) since:

- there will too many people present to enable options to be sketched up;
- design development is difficult in a formal environment;
- some design team members may comment on items outside their remit or competence (complicating the resolution of items); and
- those present may not fully understand the detail of a specific subject.

In certain circumstances, it might be advantageous to meet prior to the design team meeting to discuss and resolve a matter raised in a consultant's report so that its resolution can be reported at the meeting. If this is not possible, the lead designer should arrange a workshop so that it can be reported at the design team meeting that a technical workshop has been arranged to resolve the issue. As well as avoiding discussions in an unpredictable environment, this demonstrates that he/she is 'on top of things'.

Design workshops

If design team meetings avoid detailed design discussions, the converse is true of design workshops. However, if these workshops are to be successful they must be properly planned, chaired and the following issues considered:

- An agenda, or a list of subjects to be discussed, should be issued beforehand, and might include such matters as:
  - resolving the layout of HV/LV switchroom;
  - agreeing the strategy for bracing the building structure;
  - considering the ceiling grid and how the services might be integrated into it; or
  - determining how the lighting in a staircase might be integrated with the structure.

  There is no point in designers attending if they are not equipped with information on the agenda items.
- Numbers should be kept to a minimum. If necessary, and to keep numbers down, subject matters can be limited. Or, meetings can be rotated so that one week the emphasis is on mechanical services (at one designer's office) and the next week on structural engineering (at another designer's office). This also ensures that those designing at 'the coal face' are involved in the design development.
- Workshops should be held weekly: it is better to have a short, sharp meeting to discuss a few hot topics. However, if a specific issue is impeding the development of the design, a one-off meeting is advisable.
- Discussions should be recorded (scanned copies of sketches are adequate): future referencing may be required to enable the lead designer to demonstrate that he/she has co-ordinated the design. The design status schedule or another schedule may be used to collect and record **all** workshop issues until they are closed out. Separate minutes, or notes, become difficult to track, particularly if different subjects are discussed and different people attend each week.

The successful running of these workshops demonstrates that a truly collaborative team is in place. The main issue to consider is that, if workshops are running successfully, there will be no issues to discuss at the design team meeting! However, design team meetings can then be less reactive and more forward-looking and strategic in their outlook.

TOOL 4: PROGRESS REPORTS

Each designer must issue progress reports to the lead consultant. If the contents of these reports are properly considered they can be useful tools in resolving any design or programme issues. Conversely, if they have just been generated 'to tick a box' they will not have a constructive purpose. Progress, or status, reports are a useful tool as part of the design process because they can:

- act as a record of what each consultant has undertaken;
- allow each consultant to consider issues raised by other consultants in advance of the meeting;
- help to reduce the length of meetings;
- determine the key issues (hot topics) that exist and, if necessary, resolve them; and
- identify areas where elements of the design are behind programme and how these will be mitigated.

Reams of text setting out the items that a consultant has produced (in line with the programme) serve no purpose, whereas clear and concise text focused on the key risks and problems that are being encountered, or items that are behind programme and how these are being mitigated, provides a meaningful list of points for discussion at the meeting. If you are confident that you are managing the team effectively then you should also have confidence in a simple and informative report.

What should the format of a progress report be?

The format of the progress report should be agreed at the 'start-up' meeting and be included in the project quality plan and might consist of the following sections:

- *Previous actions* – a list of the actions assigned to the consultant at the previous meeting and their status (ideally how they have been closed out). If a specific item has not been closed out, it is essential to show that attempts have been made to progress the matter ('I have contacted X' or 'I have set up a meeting to discuss Y'). If certain parties persistently fail to conclude previous actions, the number of times that they have been carried over can be stated in the minutes.
- *Marked up programme* – a marked up (red lined) design programme is an excellent way of reporting on progress (see Figure 6.1). This allows activities that are delayed or behind programme to be recorded and methods for mitigating the delays associated with these items to be agreed and recorded in the minutes.

TOOL 4 PROGRESS REPORTS

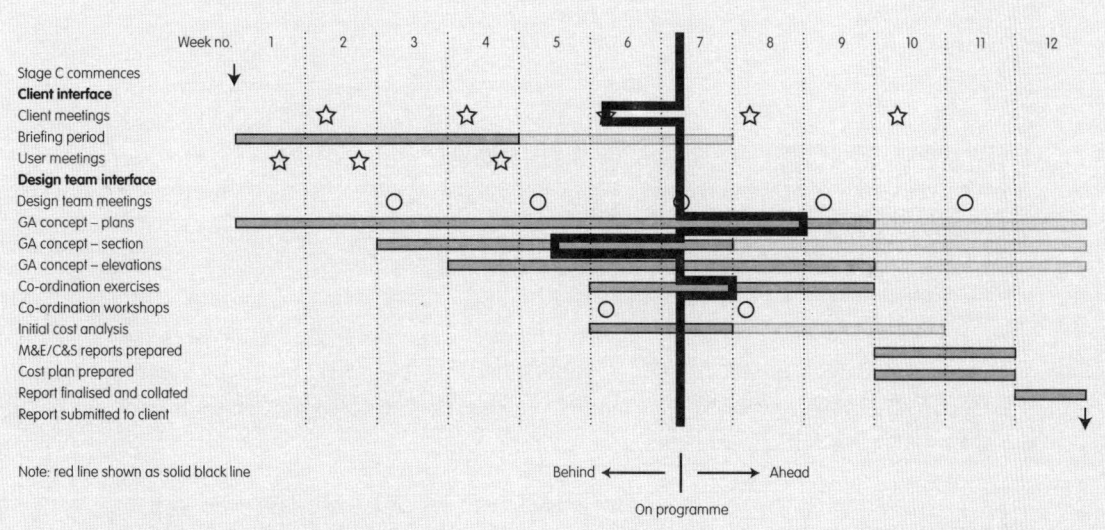

FIGURE 6.1: Red lined programme

- *Hot topics* – a list of all of the current issues that are being encountered on the project and what is required to enable these to be concluded. Ideally, these issues will have been extracted from the design status schedule (see Tool 5) or a similar log used to record the status of ongoing discussions at design workshops.
- *A look ahead* – a list of the design items that will be reviewed next and any design dependencies or risks that might revolve around these. Considering these in advance will speed up and simplify subsequent design work when it commences.
- *Statutory consents* – it is important to communicate the status of discussions, negotiations or other matters in connection with planning applications, building warrants or any other statutory consultations. A simple update on each is sufficient. Where issues do exist, for example in planning negotiations, a statement setting out how the risk is being managed can be added.
- *Health and safety* – a summary of any risks that have been identified and the status of any documentation that needs to be provided, either for statutory purposes or for other project health and safety objectives.

This format is designed to ensure that current issues are dealt with promptly (previous actions and hot topics), that any programme issues are managed and, more importantly, that, by considering forthcoming items, risks can be assessed and discussed in advance of the more significant design work that will take place.

In summary, the report should look to the future, not the past.

Why is monitoring progress against programme important?

Monitoring progress against the design programme is essential because so many design activities are dependent on the completion of others. If a design is to be completed to a satisfactory level at the end of a project stage, without caveats or incomplete elements, it is essential to consider what aspects of design have not been delivered and how these will be either brought 'up to speed' or managed. Incomplete aspects will inevitably have to be carried over to the next stage, making that stage harder to manage and deliver.

What should design team minutes contain?

Minutes should follow the format listed above and should be written in a more formal manner than discussions from a design workshop. Different practices may have different views on this subject and certain clients may also have specific formats that they wish their consultants to use.

TOOL 5: DESIGN RESPONSIBILITY MATRIX

In Chapter 3 the importance of considering the extent of contractor design on a project was considered, along with methods of determining the extent of such design works. Careful consideration, particularly from the lead designer's perspective, must also be given to the aspects of design work that might be undertaken by one designer or another: in different situations different designers might be best placed to undertake different aspects of the design.

While it is clearly best to determine such boundaries prior to design work commencing, this can be difficult when there is no design in place. However, a design responsibility matrix that deals with the typical interface issues that are encountered can still be a useful document and many practices have their own templates that they use for this purpose. Where a lead consultant regularly appoints subconsultants, it is highly recommended that a design responsibility matrix is agreed at the appointment stage in order to manage this risk.

Although the boundaries between design activities may not be clear at the beginning of the design process, they should certainly be determined and agreed by the end of stage E before each designer begins to prepare their own production information for tender purposes. Furthermore, as well as clarifying the roles of each designer, the document might also be used to set out the elements of contractor design. Clarifying who is undertaking each aspect of the design is essential prior to the tender stage. More importantly, failure to do so may result in protracted discussions on who is designing certain aspects of the design once the contractor is appointed. Such issues become more difficult to resolve once a project is underway on site and potentially result in additional costs to the client, the contractor and/or the designers. Examples of areas where ambiguities can occur include the following:

- Damp proof membrane – if a flat slab is proposed, the architect may be best placed to suggest a specification. However, if a gas-resistant membrane is required and this has interfaces between pile caps and the slab, it can be argued that the engineer should be leading the design of the membrane even if a subcontractor or supplier will provide the final solution.

TABLE 6.1: Design responsibility matrix

CLASS NOTE 1	ELEMENT	P/D NOTE 2	PSW NOTE 3	CONCEPT DESIGN
(16)	DPM	D	Yes	Arch
(21)	Brickwork	P	No	Arch
(31)	Toilet cubicles	P	No	Arch
(35)	Ceilings	D	Yes	Arch (Ser)
(43)	Carpets	P	No	Arch
(90)	Security barriers	P	No	Arch (Ser)

Arch = architect / Ser = M&E engineer / Str = C&S engineer / Con = contractor

Notes:
1. CI/FsB classification shown, but Uniclass could also be utilised.
2. Prescriptive or descriptive element.
3. Confirmation if contractor has design responsibility (Performance Specified Work).
4. Where a consultant or contractor is in brackets, this indicates a supporting role.
5. Steel lintel supports to be designed by supplier using a proprietary product. They will be specified descriptively.
6. While reference projects will be stated in the specification, the final selection of ceiling system and all support fixings will be the responsibility of the contractor.
7. Ser to design power up to agreed panel location. Con to liaise with Ser on data connections.

- The design of the gutters can be undertaken by the architect, the M&E engineer, the roofing contractor or a specialist subcontractor (for example, a contractor designing a syphonic drainage system). The lead designer must determine who is best placed to undertake this design and, vitally, when the design work is undertaken. For example, the roofing contractor may be responsible for manufacturing the gutter, but the M&E subcontractor for determining its size. If the roofing contractor's drawings are approved before the M&E contractor has determined that the size drawn is appropriate, a gutter that is inadequately sized could be put into production.

TOOL 5 DESIGN RESPONSIBILITY MATRIX

DETAIL DESIGN	FABRICATION/ SHOP DRAWINGS	APPROVAL: FIT/ APPEARANCE	ADDITIONAL NOTES
Con	Yes	Arch (Str)	Note 4
Arch (Str)	See Note 5	Arch (Str)	Note 5
Arch	Yes	Arch	–
Con	Yes	Arch (Ser)	Note 6
Arch	No	N/A	–
Con	Con	Arch (Ser)	Note 7

Ultimately, the lead consultant and the lead designer need to consider all aspects of the design and ensure that either one of the designers or the contractor is responsible for them. This is best done by setting up a matrix that clarifies which party is undertaking each aspect of the design. Typical contents of a design responsibility matrix design are shown in Table 6.1.

The first four footnotes help to clarify how the matrix is used and the last three illustrate how further clarity on aspects of potential ambiguity for specific aspects of the design can be added to the matrix.

TOOL 6: DESIGN STATUS SCHEDULE

The lead designer must consider how to demonstrate that he/she is successfully leading the design team and co-ordinating the design, and in Chapter 4 the importance of aligning design programmes with other tools in order to successfully manage the iterative stages of the design process was discussed.

Formal minutes could be used to record discussions at workshops, but they are not an effective means when different items are discussed on different occasions. Formal minutes or even notes would result in the lead designer having to monitor numerous sets of minutes with outstanding actions. To overcome this, a design status schedule can perform this task and, if properly established, this tool can also be used to perform a number of functions at different stages of the project. As well as recording discussions and agreements at design workshops, it can be used to:

- record discussions associated with the development of C&S and M&E designs, such as the development of structural grids or plantroom and riser schedules;
- demonstrate that the co-ordination of design is taking place;
- tie in with stage C programmes and record the status of key iterative elements of design;
- discuss and record cost allowances, the level of specification or design aspects where additional cost plan allowances are required;
- categorise the importance of items (hot topics);
- flag up elements where a lack of response from utilities or other third parties are preventing aspects of the design from being recorded;
- inform the contractor at tender stage of the status of the design and allow him/her to:
    - become familiarised with the status of the design and determine an appropriate level of risk in a D&B form of contract;
    - take cognisance of the elements of contractor design work and their current status; and
- register all of the design risks on the project.

TOOL 6 DESIGN STATUS SCHEDULE

If a spreadsheet format is used for generating the schedule, the following headings could be considered:

- Date item raised;
- Date item last discussed;
- Date resolution required by;
- Lead designer for item;
- Uniclass or CI/FsB, or another classification, reference;
- Level of importance (this could be aligned to hot topics).

Items would remain on the schedule until they were satisfactorily closed out and, once this had been recorded, the item would not appear on the next issue. It would be a 'live' document, being circulated on a regular basis. The spreadsheet format also allows sorting by consultant, date, hot topics or other headings that the lead designer might wish it to contain.

Depending on the size of the project, a number of schedules might be created for different purposes (for example, co-ordination or conveying design information to the cost consultant).

What are hot topics?

On any project, regardless of its size or sector there will always be a number of issues (or 'hot topics') to be resolved at a given point in time. The success of a good team leader depends on defining them, getting on top of them as promptly as possible and managing their closure as efficiently as possible. Failure to deal quickly and effectively with these issues might impact on design work and, in any event, they will not go away until they are resolved.

What might a design status schedule look like?

An example of what a design status schedule might contain is shown in Table 6.2.

TABLE 6.2: Design status schedule

DATE RAISED	LAST DISCUSSED	LEAD DESIGNER	ITEM	IMPORTANCE 1–5
13 Jan	12 Apr	Ser	HV/LV plantroom layouts	4
20 Jan	20 Jan	Str	Curtain walling support	3
23 Apr	30 Apr	Str	Bracing philosophy	3
23 Apr	30 Apr	Ser	Eaves detail	2

Arch = architect / Ser = M&E engineer / Str = C&S engineer / Con = contractor

How can health and safety considerations be imbedded into the design status schedule

Regardless of any duties contained in any appointment documents, designers have statutory obligations in relation to health and safety legislation. Due to the changing statutory environment, the specific legislative requirements are not discussed here and they are generally specific to the work of the individual designers rather than the lead consultant/designer. However, the lead designer can engender a health and safety culture on a project by:

- including health and safety as a topic on progress meeting agendas and as an item for discussion in monthly progress reports; and
- ensuring that health and safety risks are discussed at internal meetings.

Discussions and actions can then be recorded in the design status schedule.

TOOL 6 DESIGN STATUS SCHEDULE

STATUS	REQD BY	ACTION BY
Ser to provide layout of trenches to enable Str to commence prep of construction info on 3 May. Arch to check escape provision still provided	3 May	BB (Ser)
Arch to confirm setting out for CHS members in entrance that will support curtain walling	3 May	DS (Arch)
Locations of cross bracing agreed. Str to confirm member sizes to allow wall thicknesses to be finalised	7 May	AR (Str)
Ser to confirm gutter area required at eaves to enable gutter form to be drawn and steelwork to be set out	28 May	BB (Ser)

Risk management workshops

It is now customary on many projects for regular risk workshops to be undertaken and for these to be facilitated by a party from outside the team. The purpose of these workshops is to identify all of the risks on a project, assess them, and then categorise and prioritise them and assign an owner to each. Because many risks are influenced by the project programme, regular workshops are essential to ensure that the key risks are being managed and driven to a conclusion where possible. On many occasions a risk factor is determined by multiplying the impact that a risk would have on the project and multiplying that figure by the probability of the risk occurring. In some instances, spreadsheets or custom software highlight risks in green, amber or red as the risk factor increases.

The risk register (the output from risk workshops) becomes the starting point for the next workshop and, between workshops, the owners of each risk should be working towards closing them out.

TABLE 6.3: Risk schedule

DATE IDENTIFIED	RISK DESCRIPTION	LIKELIHOOD (1–10)	IMPACT (1–10)	SCORE (LXI)
Jan	HV supply	4	8	32
Feb	Planning condition 5	4	5	20
Apr	Atrium roof	2	7	14
May	Estates Committee	2	6	12
May	Road connection	3	4	12

While the key aspect of such workshops is identifying risks, in many respects the main benefit is the inclusive nature of these workshops (the client and other interested parties may be present) and the opportunity to impart to all parties the specific risks that exist in relation to what they are doing, so that each contributor is more focused on addressing their individual risks.

Although the project risk register has benefits for the project team as a whole and may have been produced by the project manager or another party, there are benefits in the lead consultant or lead designer considering how a similar register might assist in the identification of design risks. We have already suggested that the use of hot topics that are flagged up (perhaps using green, amber or red in a similar manner) in a design status schedule provides a means of prioritising critical design items. The design status schedule illustrated in Table 6.2 can be compared with the sample from a typical project risk schedule shown in Table 6.3.

TOOL 6 DESIGN STATUS SCHEDULE

RISK OWNER	RISK CATALYST	RISK CONTROL
Client	Confirmation from power company on availability	Regular chasing of power company
Architect	Approval for change from stone to render	Re-submit elevations to planners
Architect	Single supplier for proposed material	Early tender of package
Client	Estates ratify stage D after stage F commences	Change control process to assess any changes that are requested
Project manager	Completion date for road connection	Monitor council's road programme and progress

It can be concluded that there are no significant differences between the two schedules except for the scoring. With the design status schedule, the lead designer uses experience to categorise the importance of closing out issues. Whereas the risk matrix applies the combination of likelihood and the impact that any risk would have in order to determine the size of the risk. Scoring each of these categories is, however, a subjective task. It could be said that the design status is an appropriate way to manage ongoing design matters, whereas the risk matrix is of greater value for the broader project team and as a means of conveying high-risk items to the client.

TOOL 7: STRATEGIES

While drawings and specifications are the primary means of communicating the design to the client, to other designers and, ultimately, to the contractor in order to construct the works, the nature of the design process requires that detailed strategies are prepared for a number of subjects such as:

- acoustics
- fire engineering
- cleaning and maintenance
- catering
- life cycle costing
- buildability
- planning
- building control.

It is essential that the lead designer identifies the need for such strategies and who should produce them, but it is of even greater importance for him to consider:

- when these strategies will be produced;
- who will need to comment on and approve them;
- that strategies may make recommendations and not be conclusive in their findings;
- how to ensure that the rest of the design is co-ordinated to take account of the contents of the strategies; and
- the status of these strategies at tender and construction stage.

By way of example, the implications of the fire and maintenance strategies, and the issues that are typically encountered with these, are highlighted below.

Fire strategy

A fire strategy may make recommendations associated with a number of fire-related matters, such as the number of stairs, their locations and width, as well as covering compartment sizes and locations and project-specific measures, such as smoke vents at the head of the atrium. Because of the diverse nature of this strategy document, it is essential that it is not issued 'for construction'. The aspects of the report that need to be embodied within the design should be addressed by the relevant designers at stage F. So, for example, the architect should ensure that the partition drawings take due account of fire compartment walls and the M&E engineer should ensure that the ductwork drawings show fire dampers in the relevant locations. The lead designer, in checking these drawings, can compare these designs with the strategy document and also ensure that any aspects of design development have been co-ordinated. The fire strategy document may remain useful for reference purposes. However, from a construction perspective it is effectively superseded by other information

Maintenance strategy

A maintenance strategy can be a useful vehicle for demonstrating to the client the most appropriate means of maintaining and cleaning elements of the building. The strategy might, for example, show the different proposed methods for cleaning the building. These might include the use of cradle systems or a cherry picker. If the latter is proposed, the client may need to make a separate budget allowance for its purchase or an allowance in the annual maintenance budget for the rental of a machine. The strategy therefore serves a number of purposes. However, even after it has been agreed by the client, additional design and co-ordination work may be required, such as determining the location of concrete plinths, power or water supplies for a cradle system or the garage location and extent of any enhanced external paving sub-base specification for a cherry picker.

In addition, M&E items will need to be considered. For example, how are filters in the air-handling units replaced? And, if the life of the unit is less than the specified life of the building, how is the unit replaced: in sections, using the service lift, or as a single unit using a crane? Regardless, the design status schedule can be used to ensure that any design development items arising from the development, and agreement, of the strategy are managed until they are incorporated in the design.

These examples demonstrate that, as part of their co-ordination duties it is essential that the lead designer considers when the contribution of specific strategy ceases and is replaced by drawings produced by the key designers (architectural, M&E and C&S).

TOOL 8: DESIGN CHECKLISTS

The use of checklists might assist designers to determine whether all of the matters pertinent to a specific subject have been addressed or that sector-related issues have been considered. Or, they may assist someone who is reviewing information produced internally or by other designers.

The use of checklists could be part of a strategic shift in the design of buildings, where knowledge is shared for the collective use by others rather than being retained in the mind of the individual. In this regard, checklists can be a crucial part of a knowledge management system (discussed further in Chapter 9).

We have set out above how the design status schedule can be used for a number of purposes. Checklists can also perform an important role by:

- acting as a tool for younger designers by enabling them to consider all of the pertinent issues when they are progressing the design;
- providing a template for those reviewing the design to check against;
- assisting the lead designer in ensuring that elements not covered in the tender drawings or specifications are included in the design status schedule;
- enabling the designers to ensure that the cost plan includes allowance for various items that may not be considered in the early stages of the design; and
- acting as a method of disseminating the collective knowledge and experience of the designers in the office.

In terms of a classification system, Uniclass or CI/FsB might be considered but, whichever system is used, the key point will be to align all documents in any internal system to the same headings. For example, the checklist and design status schedule should use the same headings along with areas used for storing product information or other internal knowledge notes.

So, how would the checklists work?

At tender stage (the same system might be utilised at stages C and D in a simplified form) the lead designer would undertake a review of the design for each element of the building against a checklist of questions. On the basis that doors are classified as (32), Table 6.4 shows how a checklist and the resultant completed section might look. Following checklist reviews, depending on time constraints and whether the checklists have been used for reviewing internal or external information, the lead designer can

TABLE 6.4: Checklist – (32) Series: Doors

CHECKLIST ITEM	RESPONSE
Are doorsets, or doors with separate frames, proposed?	Doorsets are proposed for both steel and timber doors
Are the doors timber, metal or a combination of both?	A combination is required as indicated on door schedule
Have discussions been held with a door manufacturer?	Yes, Manufacturer X has been involved in the design development and is shown in the specification as a potential supplier
Is a door schedule available?	Door schedule included in tender pack
Does the M&E consultant require grilles in any doors or undercutting?	Some rooms require natural ventilation. M&E designer to confirm grilles required. QS to allow for cutting doors
How is the fire rating of doors covered?	The fire rating is included on the door schedule
Are vision panels required? Do these need to be fire rated?	Vision panels are required and are detailed on the door drawings. Fire rating requirements are shown on the door schedule and the QS has taken cognisance of these at stage D

Note: the above list is not meant to be definitive, but representative of how knowledge can best be managed. The response side has been completed as a project architect might respond to the knowledge queries. Subsequent issues of the design status document might close out some issues.

ensure that the design information is amended or, where this is not possible, include the reviews with the tender information or include the items in the design status schedule. The cost consultant can use the schedule to assist in the preparation of pricing or billing documents or, depending on the form of contract, the contractor can use it to make due allowances for the risks associated with the items that have been raised.

What is important is that by using the checklists, in conjunction with the design status schedule, there should be a much better understanding of the status of the design, allowing design contingencies to be calculated more accurately or for the contractor to price risk more appropriately.

By reviewing the design against a checklist, designers can also expand their knowledge by referring queries to more experienced colleagues, referring to other designers (acoustic, fire and other peripheral designers as well as the M&E and C&S engineers) or checking items with suppliers and other specialist contractors that have been involved in the development of the design.

Conclusion to Chapter 6

Eight Essential Design Management Tools

ONE — A project quality plan is required in order to establish the design team effectively from day one.

TWO — The briefing process needs to be managed to ensure that it does not significantly impact on the design process.

THREE — If amendment of the GA drawings in response to user, or other client, meetings is part of the design process, the timescales required need careful consideration.

FOUR — Design team meetings are predominately reporting meetings and should be set up and treated as such.

FIVE — Design workshops are the backbone of the co-ordination process and, while regular meetings may be advantageous, more frequent and impromptu meetings may be more effective.

SIX — Health and safety issues need to be imbedded into the design process if they are to be productive and effective.

SEVEN — Risk management techniques can be applied to the design process and developed to dovetail with the design status schedule.

EIGHT — Design checklists can provide significant advantages by providing either knowledge to designers or data to those reviewing information.

CHAPTER 7
REVIEWING DESIGN

ONE OF THE MOST IMPORTANT aspects of any design process is the verification of design work that has been undertaken. This typically occurs by reviewing, and signing-off, design information produced by consultants. Reviews generally fall into three categories:

1. Reviews where design information is presented for comment by others, including the client, planners, or local community groups. For these reviews to be successful, careful planning and preparation are required along with meticulous recording of discussions to ensure that all the pertinent issues discussed are properly dealt with. Some reviews will be milestones along the iterative design loop, others will be the formal stage reviews.
2. Reviews where design information is examined for content. This would typically be where the lead designer reviews the design work of other designers, including the architect and designing subcontractors, as part of the lead designer's duty to co-ordinate the design. The verification process may be required to adhere to practice protocols or procedures agreed and set out in the project quality plan. When specialist subcontractors produce design information this may have to be reviewed by a number of parties, which requires further consideration.
3. Internal reviews within a designer's own practice can also be beneficial and they may also have a number of functions including design control, communicating progress of projects to staff or being an integral requirement of a quality assessment (QA) system.

7.1 Why are reviews an essential part of the design process?

Before considering the issues associated with each type of review and methods of dealing with them, it is important to recognise that reviews are an essential and critical part of the design process as they:

- ensure that any interested parties have their concerns properly dealt with;
- identity risks or problems earlier in the design process, allowing them to be addressed;
- help to ensure that the work of the designers is co-ordinated;
- enable the lead consultant to demonstrate that they have fulfilled their obligations;
- allow trends across a number of projects to be identified and managed;
- can be integral to management systems;
- can demonstrate compliance with ISO standards.

In simple terms, as a design progresses, the amount of information collectively produced by the designers increases. The earlier necessary amendments are identified, the more efficient the next design stage will be for all concerned and the greater the chances of ensuring that design work is substantially complete before construction work commences on site.

7.2 How might projects benefit from internal design reviews?

A 'fresh pair of eyes' can identify aspects of the design that may not be complying with the brief or in line with best practice for a particular sector. Reviews can also ensure that the design objectives of a practice are being achieved, and identifying design issues early in the design process should result in their being dealt with more effectively and efficiently. Reviews can also benefit a project by:

- flagging up any significant flaws in a concept;
- ensuring that any sector-specific considerations have been taken into account;
- ensuring that the design is progressing in line with best practice;

- ensuring that the design is achieving the quality expected by the practice;
- identifying technical issues inherent in the design;
- harnessing the collective knowledge of a practice;
- allowing buildability or maintainability aspects to be considered;
- determining that the design can be achieved within the client's budget; and
- ensuring that any assumptions that have been made are realistic and achievable.

Reviews can be undertaken by a small group of the team leader's peers, or other senior staff experienced in the building type, or might be undertaken in a more social environment as part of a regular series of studio reviews.

As well as being beneficial to the project team, reviews can also have other practice-wide benefits, such as:

- serving as audits that demonstrate compliance with an integrated management system (IMS);
- allowing senior staff to have an overview of the many projects which may be in development; and
- enabling any significant issues to be dealt with before the design progresses too far.

Why are internal design reviews difficult to organise?

Internal design reviews, particularly in a busy design studio, are difficult to plan as the mantra 'hasta mañana' is frequently used when an internal session is proposed. Client presentations cannot be avoided, but peer reviews are often perceived as an unnecessary additional deadline and it is inevitable that they will have to be scheduled between major client deadlines (when the design might be in a state of flux), before a client meeting (where negative feedback might demoralise the team) or following a client meeting (when other issues will be fresh in the minds of the team). In short, there is never a good time for internal reviews! Yet, peer reviews can provide many benefits for a project team which might not be able to 'see the wood for the trees'.

7.3 What is the purpose of management reviews?

In addition to design reviews, regular reviews of the management aspects of a project can identify management risks and ensure that they are promptly addressed and resolved. They can also be used to identify trends occurring across a number of projects, allowing internal processes to be continuously improved. In some practices, such undertakings may be a requirement of the practice's QA or IMS procedures or other internal processes.

Even if they are not formalised, a good team leader will undertake regular reviews of the project with the director, partner or practice leader responsible for the project.

What aspects might a management review cover?

The subjects covered by a management review might be determined by specific practice protocols and procedures, but might include:

- the status of appointment documents, including subconsultant appointments, and any issues that are preventing these from being concluded;
- invoicing and payment of invoices;
- change control;
- a review of the project programme, including project milestones, and any issues arising from this;
- project spend and performance;
- project resource issues; and
- project hot topics and how they are being dealt with.

If these reviews are to be successful, they need to work in conjunction with other management systems. For example, how is the financial performance of a project communicated to the team leaders on a regular basis and what other means are used to manage and resolve practice-wide resource issues?

Successfully undertaking reviews will assist the smooth and efficient running of projects by ensuring that appointment documents are timeously concluded, identifying and resolving potential management issues promptly and, when the same senior staff members are undertaking a number of reviews, trends occurring from project to project can be identified for consideration at senior management meetings (addressing both positive and negative observations).

7.4 Reviewing information from other consultants?

Before considering the issues associated with reviewing the work of other consultants, it is essential to consider the obligations stated in the RIBA appointment. For the lead consultant role it states:

> 'With the Contract Administrator/Employer's Agent, Lead Designer and CDM-Co-ordinator co-ordinating and reviewing the work of consultants and site inspectors after stage G.'

The lead designer is involved in this duty; however, the lead designer's main duty in relation to the design work of other designers is:

> 'Co-ordinating design of all <u>constructional</u> elements, including work by consultants, specialists or suppliers and for health and safety matters in conjunction with CDM-C.'

From these obligations it can be concluded that the lead designer's review of other designers' work is not an obligation in the early stages of the design: it is only a necessity after stage G. In many respects this is sensible because, in the majority of instances, design programmes cannot accommodate the time required to review other designers' information in the earlier project stages and, in reality, a number of methods need to be used to co-ordinate the design. Besides, the lead designer will have been co-ordinating the design in the early stages of the project and the principles agreed should appear on each designer's drawings.

However, the lead designer must bear in mind that, unless the outputs of the designers are reviewed, there is no guarantee that this co-ordination work has been manifested in the designers' outputs. The implications of this need to be considered, particularly in relation to the procurement route as changes required as a result of checking any drawings may incur additional costs after the project has been tendered.

It is essential to ensure that any production information being issued after stage G (i.e. for construction purposes) by any designer has been reviewed as part of the final co-ordination of design work before it is either used on site to construct the works or by specialist subcontractors to produce their design information: co-ordination issues are better identified on drawings than on site. In this regard, the time taken to review information **must** be included in any design programmes.

LEADING THE TEAM

The lead designer must also consider how subsequent issues of information are to be handled. Establishing a review process for every issue of a drawing might be counterproductive, and it is likely that subsequent revisions will impact ongoing work on site and will therefore need to be issued quickly.

Who should review consultant information?

Reviews can be undertaken by members of a team who have been instrumental in the co-ordination of the design and who understand the strategies that have been developed, as well as by specialist reviewers who can look at the design holistically and impartially. Where the lead designer is also a designer (typically the architect), the points made below will also apply to the review of design information produced by the lead designer's internal architectural team.

What has to be considered when reviewing consultant information?

When reviewing information, the following points must be considered if the reviews are to be successful, particularly when items are identified during the review process:

- The information should be reviewed against design decisions that have been agreed at design workshops and information contained in the completed, and signed off, stage D or E reports.
- Information should be reviewed against other relevant information, which might include:
  - fire strategy reports,
  - acoustic reports,
  - Building Regulations,
  - British, or European, Standards, and
  - sector-specific guidance such as health technical memorandums (HTMs) used in the healthcare sector.
- Reviews may need to be undertaken simultaneously: for example, ensuring that the structural information for an electrical substation is in accordance with the requirements of the M&E designer's information.
- Reviews should consider aspects of maintenance. For example, when checking mechanical drawings that show valves, dampers, transformers or other concealed elements, the lead designer should consider whether the

architectural design includes for the demountable ceilings, riser doors and/or access hatches necessary to access these components for maintenance.
- Reviews should not be used to change design direction. Change control should be used if reviews determine that an alternative design strategy is more appropriate.
- The project quality plan should set out how reviews will be undertaken and comments should be communicated back to the originating designer. Drawings are typically marked up by the designer(s), either using red pen or, increasingly, electronically.
- Comments need to be clear and objective. If too many subjective comments are being made (such as 'Can this be moved over here?' or 'Can this beam be smaller?'), it may be necessary to hold a workshop to resolve these issues.
- Allowances must be made in the design programme for undertaking reviews and for the time required by each designer to amend their information in line with any comments that have been made. As noted above, this will be essential for construction information; however, at tender stage the pros and cons of undertaking reviews, along with any obligations in appointments documents, need to be considered.
- Finally, because comments that are made on construction information may impact work on site, it is essential to have a proactive approach to resolving such comments, rather than just returning comments on a drawing and placing the onus on the relevant designer to resolve the issue. Instead, the problems should be flagged up immediately and a workshop held to resolve them.

How does reviewing relate to the co-ordination process?

Reviewing is an activity that should ratify whether the co-ordination process has been properly undertaken by the lead designer. It should not be used to carry out co-ordination (although it is inevitable that minor design issues will be identified during the process).

Chapter 3 set out some of the steps taken at each stage to produce a co-ordinated design but, in addition to these, the lead designer should consider what other workshops might be held to ensure that, when drawings on a particular aspect of the design are received for reviewing, they do not contain any surprises. For example:

- Has a workshop been held with the M&E designer to discuss the light fittings, grilles and other visible elements that are to be specified?

LEADING THE TEAM

- If specific connections are required for visible steelwork elements, have these been discussed with the C&S designer and agreement reached on how the elements might be detailed?

In summary, reviewing drawings should be the final part of the co-ordination process, not part of the iterative design process. Indeed, to leave such exercises too late in the design process could result in a significant amount of uncoordinated information being issued for tender (increasing the contractor's risk or requiring subsequent instructions depending on the procurement route) or to site (where subsequent amendments to constructed work may be required).

If the consultants are employed as subconsultants, does it change the review process?

In situations where a consultant is employed as a subconsultant there is no reason why the checking processes outlined above should be altered. However, it has to be remembered that a subconsultant error could result in a claim by the client on the lead consultant.

If a practice's turnover has a significant proportion of subconsultant work there may be benefits, from a risk management perspective, in employing a specialist with an M&E or C&S design background to review design information. Alternatively, a second technical review or a review undertaken in a workshop environment by a number of the lead designer's peers might be considered and both would be viable ways of reducing this risk.

In the next section the categorisation of specialist subcontractor's drawings is considered and, although it is not standard within the industry at present, a similar system for subconsultant drawings might provide a better focus as follows:

- Category A – can be issued for construction;
- Category B – can be issued for construction if minor amendments, in line with comments, are made;
- Category C – cannot be issued for construction until the comments raised have been discussed and addressed.

Such an approach would make the lead designer's position on a particular drawing clear.

7.5 Reviewing specialist subcontractor design

In the previous section, it was noted that the process of reviewing other consultants' design work should confirm that the information is in line with co-ordination decisions that have already been made. The same principle applies to specialist subcontractor design information. Chapter 3 set out how design intent information can be used to ensure that the co-ordination of adjacent elements is considered and, by utilising pre- and post-tender meetings, the principles of any key co-ordination issues, which might arise from the development of the subcontractor design, can be addressed before the contract has been awarded to the specialist subcontractor with any residual issues recorded in the design status schedule.

Furthermore, because any residual design issues that arise can be dealt with during regular workshops that will be organised and chaired by the contractor there should, in principle, be very few comments to make on the subcontractor's design drawings.

What needs to be considered when reviewing subcontractor design information?

When reviewing the design information of specialist subcontractors, the comments made in the last section are all of equal validity. In addition, there are several other significant factors that must be taken into consideration:

- The specialist subcontractor can only base his/her drawings on the information provided. If this information is incorrect, the subcontractor drawings will also be incorrect (although any anomalies may be identified and rectified during the subcontractor's design process). Therefore, when checking drawings, consider how diligently your own package of information has been prepared. Was it rushed for a deadline? Did you rigorously check your information? Was it checked thoroughly by someone else? If, after considering these points, you have any doubts, then a careful check of the contractor's drawings, particularly in relation to setting out, is recommended: better spending a few extra minutes checking drawings than the hours, and probably significant cost, of adjusting a prefabricated component that arrives on site and does not fit.
- The checking process should **never** be used to change what was included on the design intent drawings. For example, making a flashing 100 mm deeper

because it 'looks better' is a change of scope and will incur additional costs. The change control process should be used and the designer's drawings amended and reissued as necessary if the change is accepted by the client.
- Likewise, design intent drawings should **never** be amended to reflect the detailed information on the contractor's design drawings. The design intent drawings are, effectively, superseded by the contractor's drawings. The only exception is where the design work of one element impacts on that of another, requiring the interface to be amended. For example, if the development of the curtain walling impacts on the brickwork design, the brickwork aspect of the drawing should be amended. However, if the curtain walling designer requires adjustments to elements that only impact on his/her own works, the design intent drawings would remain unchanged.

Returning subcontractor drawings

It is now standard procedure to return specialist subcontractor design drawings with a category assigned. These categories are usually defined in the tender preliminaries and have been developed to ensure that there are no ambiguities regarding the status of a drawing. The categories are:

- Category A – fabrication and/or construction can commence;
- Category B – fabrication and/or construction can commence once information has been amended in line with minor comments; and
- Category C – fabrication and/or construction cannot commence.

Each specialist contractor should produce their own design programme showing design workshops and the periods when drawings will be issued. More importantly, subcontractor programmes must allow for a number of iterations of the drawings (Category A is not always achieved on the first issue) and for the subsequent amendments and reissue of the drawings.

The lead designer must also remember that, while there may be no specific obligation to return drawings within a specified timeframe, the prelims will state that the specialist subconsultant must receive comments back within a period of time (typically ten days from the date on which the reviewer received the drawings) and that any delays may result in progress on site being delayed and the subcontractor making a claim for an extension of time.

Finally, in some instances a number of designers may need to make comments on a particular subcontractor's set of information. These comments may have to be co-ordinated before the drawings are returned. The method of achieving this (and monitoring to ensure that it occurs) within the ten-day period can present a number of management challenges and should ideally be considered at the start of the project when the project quality plan is being prepared and the scope of contractor design is being agreed.

Conclusion to Chapter 7
Reviewing Design

ONE   Designers must properly prepare for any external meetings where other parties will be reviewing their design work.

TWO   Internal reviews can usefully identify design issues or confirm that the design is proceeding in the right direction.

THREE   Internal management reviews can ensure that contract documentation is being concluded and act as a forum to consider project issues such as progress and resources.

FOUR   Internal management reviews can identify trends that are occurring across any projects and allow practice-wide processes to be amended in response to any feedback.

FIVE   Reviewing other designers' drawings should confirm that they have taken account of the co-ordination exercises that have already taken place.

SIX   Checking of specialist contractor drawings is made easier when interfaces and other issues have been considered at an earlier design stage.

SEVEN   The method for a number of designers to comment on a specialist subcontractor's design should be agreed and included in the project quality plan.

CHAPTER 8
HOW PROCUREMENT AFFECTS THE DESIGN MANAGEMENT CHALLENGE

CHAPTER 3 CONSIDERED the subject of contractor design and how this design work might be managed. However, the form of procurement selected for a project places design responsibility on different parties and it is important for the lead consultant and lead designer to consider how the selected procurement route (they may be party to the decision) might impact on the design process and the obligations and liabilities that might be involved.

8.1 How might the selected procurement route impact on the design process?

Although there is sufficient collective experience of different procurement routes, deciding on the most appropriate procurement route can still be difficult for those involved. While time, cost and quality are the key drivers for determining the most appropriate route, design matters should also influence any such decision. From a design perspective, the variables which differ in each of the procurement models include:

- when the contractor's involvement in the design process commences;
- what degree of influence the contractor has over the design process;
- what contribution the contractor is able or is required to make to the design as it develops;
- the extent of contractor design work to be undertaken; and
- which party takes responsibility for each aspect of the design.

LEADING THE TEAM

While the work undertaken might ultimately be the same, different procurement routes might vary the timing and amount of production information that is produced for tender and, in order manage the design process, the lead consultant/designer must understand the implications of this and the impact on, and risks to, the design process.

It is important to remember that contractor design forms of procurement were introduced because clients:

- wanted to enter into contracts with a fixed cost and completion date for a given design;
- saw the benefits of a single focal, and contractual, point for any construction or design issues; and/or
- believed that an earlier contribution from the contractor, when designers were making significant design decisions, would result in more cost-effective buildings.

What risks might occur as a result of the chosen procurement route?

The design process begins with sketch designs which are developed and enhanced until a completed set of construction documents is produced. The steps in between the start and the end can vary, particularly in relation to the production of stage E and F information, and may be dependent on the procurement route and form of building contract that is selected. The lead consultant/designer must consider the following issues.

- *Early contractor involvement* – on some forms of procurement the contractor may be appointed early in the design process and Figure 8.1 illustrates the RIBA stages at which the contractor's involvement may commence. On a complex project where specialised or innovative design solutions are being considered, this can greatly assist the lead designer by allowing buildability and programming considerations to be considered in parallel with the design process. On more straightforward projects, the contractor may try to review decisions already made by the consultants and may also wish to progress design aspects more quickly than the design process allows while not distracted by the main role of constructing the project. To overcome this, the timing and need for any pre-commencement contractor duties must be carefully considered. Where the contractor has such duties, a design programme is essential to ensure that the design process is not unnecessarily impeded.

CHAPTER 8 PROCUREMENT

```
                    RIBA stages
                    ┌───┐
                    │A/B│
                    └───┼───┐
                        │ C │
                        └───┼───┐
                            │ D │
                            └───┼─────┐
                                │ E/F1│
                                └─────┼─────┐
                                      │ G/H │
                                      └─────┼────────┐
                                            │F2/J/K  │
                                            └────────┼───┐
                                                     │ L │
                                                     └───┘
```

Type of contract

Traditional

Design & Build – 1 stage | Note 1

Design & Build – 2 stage | Note 2

Management contract | Note 2

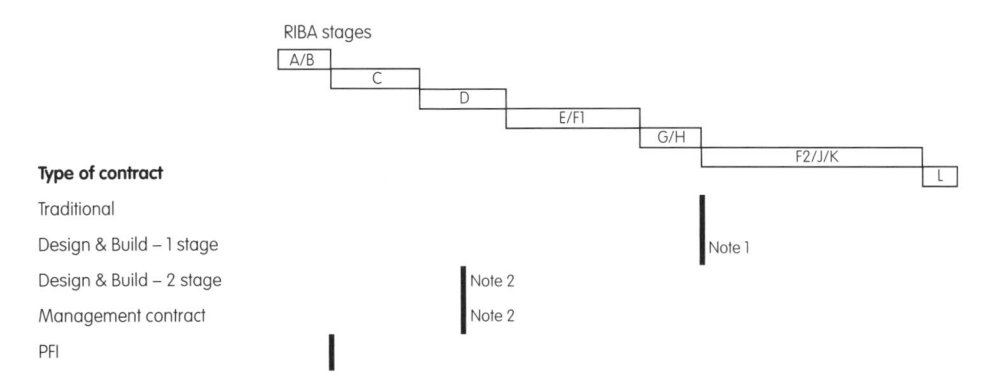

PFI |

Note 1: The amount of F1 work is likely to be less than a traditional contract but will vary from project to project
Note 2: The contractor will have tendered on the basis of profit, prelims and overhead

FIGURE 8.1: When does the contractor get involved?

KEY TERM   **Employer's requirements** the set of documents on which the contractor will base the tender. These can vary from a simple statement to a comprehensive set of drawings and specifications.

KEY TERM   **Contractor's proposals** the set of documents that will form the basis of the contract between the client and the contractor. These might consist of design proposals prepared by the contractor's own consultants or a marked up set of the employer's requirements.

• *Transfer/allocation of risk* – the employer's requirements and the contractor's proposals are key contract documents. It is essential that the lead consultant/designer is aware of the contents of both and has assisted the risk transfer process by providing a design status schedule. For remeasurable contracts it is essential that the lead consultant/designer is aware of the contingency allowances that are available for completing aspects of the design (he/she may have ensured that appropriate provisional sums have been included in the tender).

On D&B contracts, the potential for disputes between the designers and the contractor can be minimised, and managed, by ensuring that the contractor is fully aware of the design status before entering into a contract. This is of particular importance where the designers are to be novated. Lack of dimensions will not impact on cost; however, lack of drawings or a failure to describe a particular design feature may have significant cost implications. Statements on co-ordination or incomplete aspects of the design can be included in the design status schedule, which is discussed in greater detail in Chapter 6: Eight essential design management tools.

LEADING THE TEAM

No matter what form of procurement was used, it is likely that the same parties will have **undertaken** the same design work. However, it is the contractual matrix that will allocate the **responsibility** of this design work to the different parties.

In addition to the issues set out above, each procurement route has further subtle nuances that may impact on the design process, and some of these issues and how they might impact on the design process are considered below. Documents such as the JCT's *Deciding on the appropriate JCT contract* also cover these aspects in greater detail.

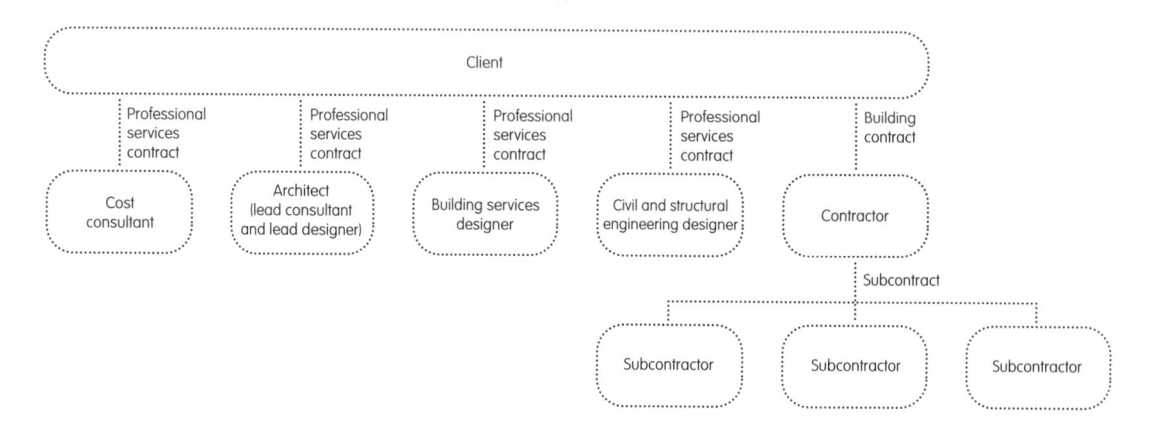

FIGURE 8.2: Traditional procurement route – contractual structure

Traditional procurement

In a traditional procurement route, responsibility for the design will rest entirely with the design team who are employed by the client, although discrete elements of the design may be allocated to the contractor using contractor design versions of standard contracts. Figure 8.2 illustrates the typical make up of the team under a traditional contract.

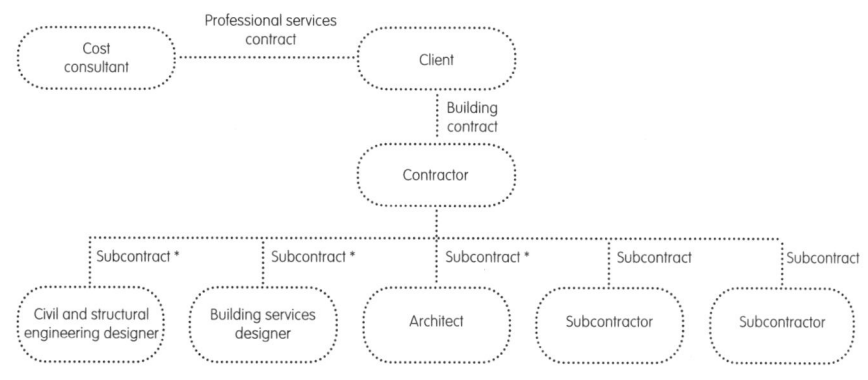

FIGURE 8.3: D&B procurement route – contractual structure

Design and build

On design and build forms of procurement, the contractor typically accepts full responsibility for all aspects of the design. Even when a contractor is responsible for the design, it is likely that the majority of the design work will be undertaken by a consultant or a subcontractor employed by the contractor. In some forms of design and build the consultants, originally employed by the client, are novated to the contractor. In these instances, designers should ensure that their post-novation responsibilities and duties are clearly stated in their appointment.

KEY TERM **Novation** on many D&B projects the consultants are novated to the contractor. The concept of novation is simple: the contractor replaces the original client in the appointment and, from that point forward, the consultant's obligations and duties are to the contractor, not the original client. The contractor becomes the consultant's client. Following novation, designers must ensure that direct communication with the original client ceases and is directed through the new client: the contractor. Failure to do so may result in the designer breaching his/her obligations to the new client. It is often the case that designers will be responsible to the contractor for all of the design work undertaken prior to novation. The designers should be aware that they may be liable for any issues that arise post-novation in relation to an error in the pre-novation design (which the contractor has relied on in preparing the tender). Figure 8.3 illustrates how this form of procurement affects the contractual relationship between the various parties.

Two-stage design and build

In many respects, two-stage D&B combines the programme advantages of management contracting (see below) with the time and cost benefits of D&B forms of contract, as well as creating a single point of accountability. In some instances, the specialist subcontractor design work may be completed before the contractor enters into the contract and, while this minimises the contractor's risk from the designer's perspective, the design programme, for the issue of tender and construction information to specialist subcontractors, is likely to be more onerous because:

- tender information for the majority of the design will be required early in the design process to assist the contractor in concluding the contract sum;
- early packages will require construction information to be issued to site (contractors typically carry out early packages under a letter of intent);
- the co-ordination of C&S and M&E tender information will have to be undertaken in parallel; and
- design workshops and checking of subcontractor drawings will be taking place for the design work of specialist subcontractors who have already been appointed.

The challenges of dealing with many aspects of subcontractor design in these early stages can be significant.

Single stage design and build

As noted above, on a two-stage D&B project the majority of specialist subcontractor design can be completed and agreed **before** a contract is agreed with the client and, possibly, before work progresses on site. On a single stage D&B, this design work will be completed **after** the contract is agreed and it is not therefore possible to conclude subcontractor design issues until the contractor is appointed and the team novated (if this is to occur).

Due to the likely pressures to start as early as possible on site after the award date, and the need, on contract award, to catch up with the design work of specialist subcontractors, it is essential that a design programme, for the release of construction information, is agreed as part of the tender process. This is covered further in Chapter 4: Programming design.

Management contracting

Management contracting was developed in order to deliver commercial buildings to the market as quickly as possible. This was achieved by compressing the project programme as much as possible and significantly overlapping design and construction. Following stage D, the management contractor allocates the different elements of the design into 'packages', with each package or 'trade contract' put out to tender and awarded individually. The design programme is determined by working backwards from the completion date and the construction and procurement programmes. This has a significant impact on the design process because:

- the first elements of design are issued shortly after planning consent is granted;
- some elements are designed out of their logical design sequence;
- the design work of different designers takes place concurrently, making co-ordination difficult;
- design work of specialist subcontractors may impact on work that is already co-ordinated;
- design work continues for a significant part of the construction period; and
- tendering elements in packages requires a detailed consideration of interfaces between different elements of construction.

Designers must understand how to design out of sequence: issuing construction information for one package one day and sketching early design details for another package the next day. The concept of design intent information was created to allow specialists to tender on a competitive basis, yet allowing different systems or solutions to be considered. Performance specifications, which are now used in most procurement routes, were also created to facilitate this process.

Private Finance Initiative (PFI)

On PFI projects, the design team is appointed by the contractor from the outset as part of the contractor's bid team. The contractor will be influential in the development of the design from the commencement of the project and will also be responsible for this design. Good design is essential if such bids are to be successful. This is generally recognised by contractors and they play a key role in the management of the design process by ensuring good engagement with client user groups and the early involvement of their supply chain subcontractors. This ensures that best value is being achieved. A further benefit is that a facilities management (FM) company will be a member of the contractor's bid team (often a special purpose vehicle (SPV) created to bid for the project) and, as such, life cycle aspects will be considered in greater detail. Increasingly, this form of procurement is being described as contractor-led design, which is a more accurate and appropriate term.

The design issues involved in PFI projects are similar to those of a two-stage D&B or management contracting contract; but, as the contractor is involved from the outset, specialist contractor input, including cost information, can be obtained earlier in the design process in order to assist the development of the design. The contractor can also utilise the specialist subcontractor supply chain to establish costs, rather than go through a tendering process, creating a less onerous peak of design activity at the front end. However, if the contractor is successful, the front-end packages will have to be concluded rapidly to allow work to progress on site. The major design consideration is that all communication with the client regarding design decisions must be undertaken in the presence of the contractor's representative.

Conclusion to Chapter 8

How Procurement Affects the Design Management Challenge

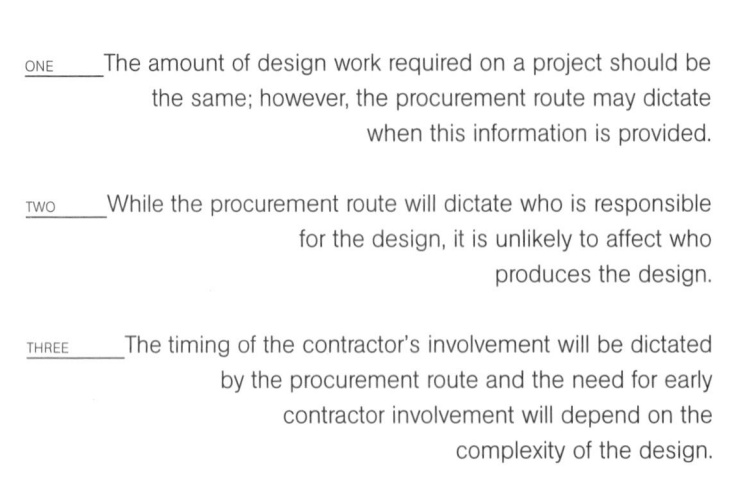

ONE   The amount of design work required on a project should be the same; however, the procurement route may dictate when this information is provided.

TWO   While the procurement route will dictate who is responsible for the design, it is unlikely to affect who produces the design.

THREE   The timing of the contractor's involvement will be dictated by the procurement route and the need for early contractor involvement will depend on the complexity of the design.

CHAPTER 9
STREAMLINING PRACTICE MANAGEMENT

CHAPTER 6 ESTABLISHED the benefits of using design management tools to assist the management of the design process. We will now consider what management systems and techniques might be applied practice-wide, or used by a team leader on an individual project to improve these processes still more.

You may feel that these topics are too management orientated and that, while they are relevant to the practice as a whole, they are not of concern to your own busy project team. But remember that each can add value to the design process, resulting in more efficient projects, a better-run practice and, more importantly, greater success in securing new work.

Such systems are also of particular importance to those involved in tendering for public-sector design work in response to European Journal notices. With these bids it is becoming more common for detailed questions on numerous subjects to be included within prequalification questionnaires (PQQs) or in subsequent bid stages. An understanding and knowledge of the concepts set out in this chapter therefore allow responses to be made in a more considered manner and may also dictate changes to a number of internal processes including:

- quality assurance processes;
- continual improvement;
- benchmarking;
- post-occupancy evaluation;
- resource management;
- knowledge management;
- risk management.

9.1 Quality assurance processes

Many practices have quality assurance (QA) systems with most of these adhering to the requirements of ISO 9001: 2008 and achieving accreditation from a third party. The key attributes will be:

- established procedures and processes that are audited;
- verification procedures;
- continual improvement.

The best systems will be embodied within the culture of a practice, with external auditing requiring no additional efforts from any members of staff in advance of audits. Some systems might be internally branded, as part of a knowledge management system or culture, and may require 'translation' documents, such as a process manual that acts as a bridge between QA-speak and the straightforward language preferred by designers.

Continual improvement, covered in detail in the next section, is a relatively new requirement of ISO 9001: 2008, but can be of significant importance to designers.

9.2 Continual improvement

Continual improvement is essential if a practice is to increase its effectiveness and become more efficient. In the context of more competitive fees, more demanding clients and increasing legislative requirements, improved performance is imperative if new projects are to be secured, run profitably and to enable a practice to maintain its competitive edge.

Of course, in order to improve, an established means of working or set of procedures need to be in place. The majority of practices have such processes in place and an effective team leader will understand how these work and how they relate to and conform to industry-wide norms. At the outset of a project, any changes to these processes, driven by the appointment documentation, or specific project demands, can be determined, agreed and set out in the project quality plan.

If a practice does not have established procedures it is clearly difficult to make improvements. With established procedures it is far easier to make suggestions that will fine-tune and improve the internal processes that exist. Feedback can be gleaned on an

CHAPTER 9 STREAMLINING PRACTICE MANAGEMENT

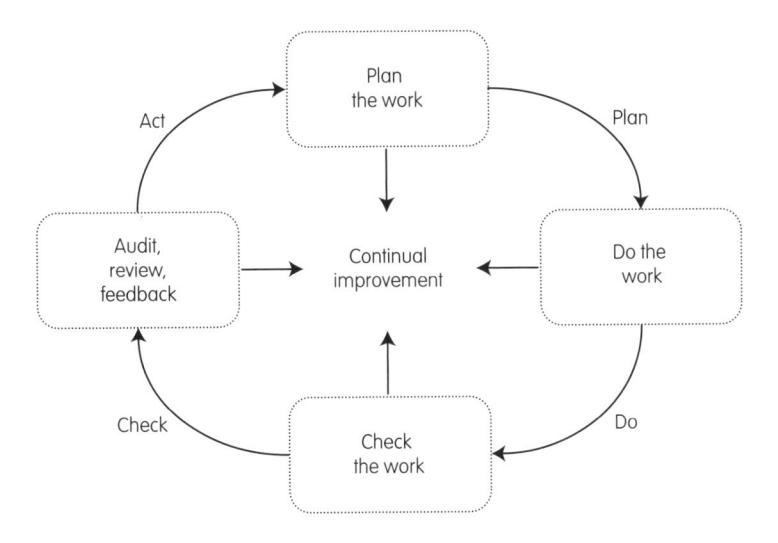

FIGURE 9.1: Continual improvement

ongoing basis, using key performance indicators (KPIs) or post-occupancy evaluations (POEs). These two subjects are covered in the next two sections.

Continual improvement (see Figure 9.1) is focused on increasing the efficiency and effectiveness of a practice in order to fulfil its policy and objectives. As well as quality initiatives, to improve business results, customer and employee relationships can also be subject to continual improvement. Put simply, continual improvement means getting better all the time and:

- should focus on all areas of a practice's business, including practice structure, leadership, communication, staff, resources and project or business processes – in other words, every aspect of the practice;
- can lead to better results such as increased profit, reduced costs, and improved customer and employee satisfaction;
- requires measurement, as there can be no improvement without this. An organisation must establish current performance before embarking on any improvement. If it does not, it will have no baseline from which to determine if its efforts have yielded any improvement; and
- benefits from established improvement cycles: gateway reviews may take place but, as a minimum, an end of project review should be established (see next section).

The cultural attitudes required to enable collaborative working are similar to those needed to achieve continual improvement: resistance to change or the defence of the status quo cannot result in improvement. A means of congratulating those who achieve significant improvement is essential and the subject can perhaps be covered, along with the best improvements that have been implemented, at office meetings.

Reference is sometimes made to other methods of continuous improvement, such as lean thinking, Six Sigma or total quality management (TQM) and further research on these will provide additional understanding of this subject.

9.3 Benchmarking (KPIs)

If continual improvement is to be successful, performance has to be measured. Statistics about performance are clearly easier to obtain in manufacturing businesses, where targets are simpler to record (number of widgets installed per hour, number of faulty assembled widgets per 1000) and in such businesses this information may have been produced for decades, allowing the benefits of new computerised plant systems or new processes to be properly understood.

Design, of course, is different because so many aspects of design are subjective. However, there are various items that can be measured on a project and business level, and a number of initiatives are taking place in an attempt to make available more historical data. This includes the RIBA benchmark study that makes key business information available annually, allowing practices to understand their performance in relation to their peers.

At a project level, CABE have introduced a design quality indicator (DQI), which is a means of evaluating the design and construction of a building. Figure 9.2 is representative of the output that arises from the use of structured workshops and the online tools that are available.

While these diagrams are useful and begin to provide benchmarking data, it must be remembered that the scoring is subjective and, while general trends might be identified (for example, all buildings scoring poorly on lighting), the specific data for individual buildings should be treated with caution.

Constructing Excellence has also produced a number of benchmarking tools to enable business performance on items such as profitability and overhead recovery rates to be mapped on their comparative schedules.

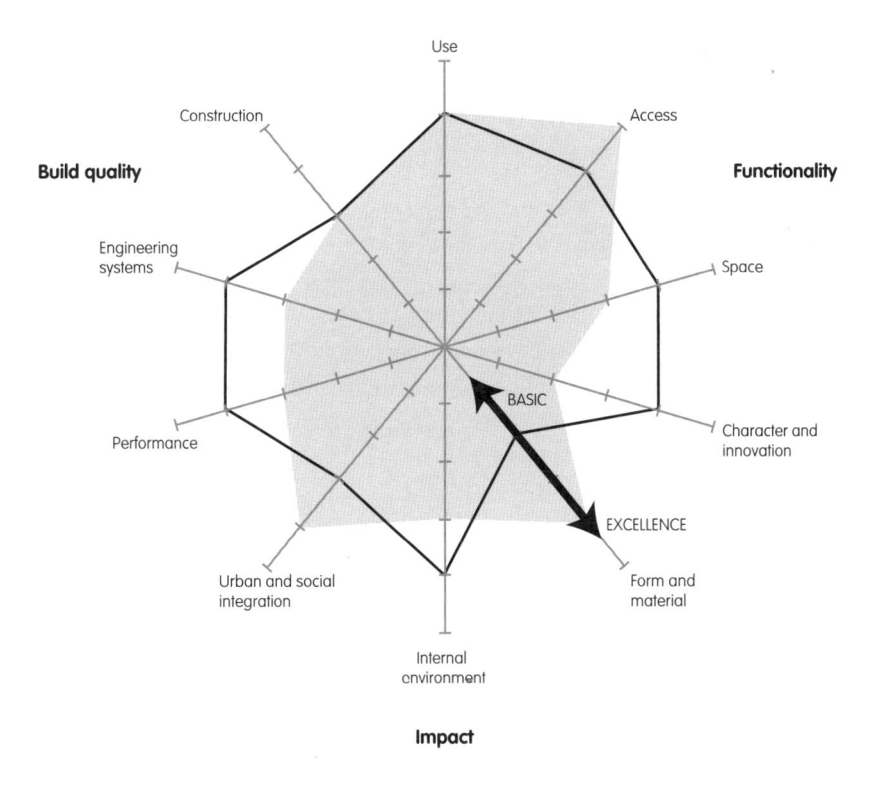

FIGURE 9.2: Design quality indicator

Project statistics can be used to:

- establish resource profiles at the beginning of projects based on historical data;
- determine the percentage of actual spend at each RIBA stage on previous projects;
- inform the project architect on how the project is performing against the plan;
- allow completed resource profiles to be compared (why did a project exceed its resource budget?) with historical ones; and
- assist the design process (by comparing net to gross ratios or cost per square metre).

When project and business data are collated they can be used as part of an annual business review and may assist in setting targets for the following year (or as part of a five-year business plan). The following data might be gathered:

- net/gross profit;
- turnover;

- job profit;
- range of project sizes.

Other data might assist in the development of a practice's marketing strategy:

- fees secured by sector;
- fees secured by region (which might include countries); or
- fees secured by value (or construction value).

In conclusion, if the potential uses of benchmark data can be determined, their annual collation can begin. Data can be used for many purposes; however, the longer the period over which the data has been prepared, the easier it is to see trends and to respond to these accordingly.

9.4 Post-occupancy evaluation (POE)

POEs are an increasingly used tool in the construction industry, and the subject is of particular interest to those who build many buildings, perhaps as part of an estate, such as a university or hospital trust. The contents and specific benefits of a post-occupancy evaluation will depend on when it is held in relation to the project's completion and occupation by the client.

On completion

Following completion, a POE allows the design team and the client, along with other participants, to discuss the successes and failures of the design and construction phases of the project. It is inevitable that both successes and failures will have occurred and it is important that any session dwells on both and not exclusively on one or the other. The outcomes of such sessions can be invaluable in addressing process or procedural aspects. Some of the issues may relate to a clash of personalities. These can be dealt with at the annual appraisal of the relevant team member.

Six months or longer after occupation

After the building has been operational for a number of months or years, the emphasis of POEs will be on communicating how various aspects of the building have performed and, where appropriate, discussing aspects of the design that have been both successful and unsuccessful, in order to provide a balanced overview.

9.5 Resource management

The biggest single item of expenditure for any design practice is staff salaries, and management of this resource is one of the most difficult aspects of running a practice. It is not possible to consider the holistic issues of resource management in this section; it is, however, worthwhile to look at project-specific resourcing issues. These should be straightforward: a resource plan is produced, checked against the fee and then monitored monthly in order to ensure that no overspend is occurring. If overspend is occurring, a contingency allowance can be utilised. It is also important to consider whether progress is ahead of or behind the planned percentage completion. In any case, close management is required to ensure that a project does not become loss making.

The key elements to consider when producing a resource plan are:

- Programme – resource requirements are particularly sensitive to programme as it is a human trait that if we are given six weeks to complete a task that requires four weeks, we will take six weeks. More demanding programmes, while creating significant pressure on a project team, can be more profitable. Figure 9.3 illustrates a typical resource profile for a traditional project; however, stage E/F has been compressed slightly and the chart reflects the larger team required to accommodate this.
- Benchmarking – historical resourcing information can provide a useful basis for the resource profile of a project. If this is not available, then data on how fees have been spent by each RIBA stage, along with copies of previous strategic programmes, may allow trends to be identified. In the absence of such information altogether, resource profiles, or plans, can only be based on past experience (tacit knowledge) or estimated.
- Staff allocation – aside from the lead members of staff, who typically work on a number of projects, staff should not be allocated for 50 or 80 per cent of their

LEADING THE TEAM

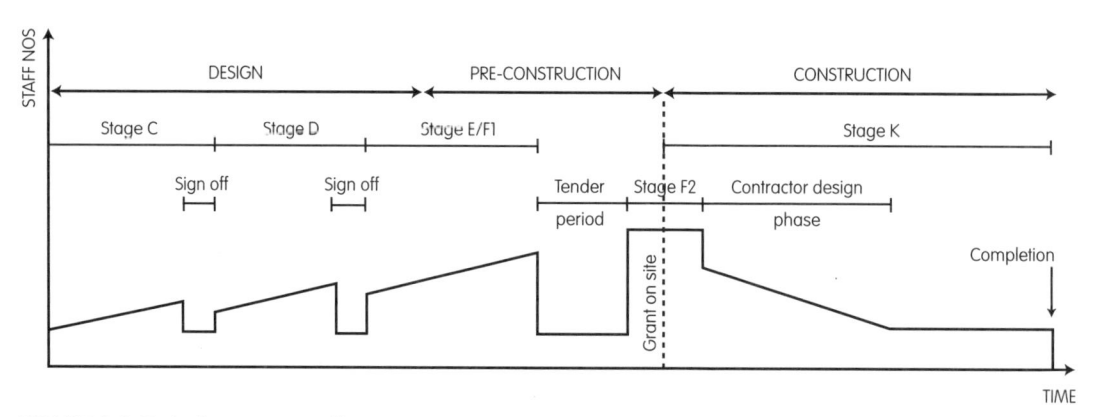

FIGURE 9.3: Typical resource profile

time in order to make the numbers work. It is inevitable that most members of your team will be working full time so such techniques will inevitably lead to the project overspending and becoming less profitable. It is better to allocate staff full time and then try to ensure that they complete their tasks within the timescale that the practice can afford.

- Contingency – it is important to allow a budget within the overall fee (along with allowances for non-reimbursable expenses and profit) that can be utilised for additional resources during a project 'hot spot' or at the end of a specific stage. If these resources are not required, then the project becomes more profitable.

While preparing a resource plan, a detailed knowledge of the fee is not essential. Indeed, it could be argued that if the resource plan is properly benchmarked it can be prepared in isolation. However, when the resource plan has been completed and costed, it should be compared against the proposed or even agreed fee. If the fee covers the anticipated resources and also leaves sufficient allowances for expenses, inflation, an element of contingency and profit, it is likely that the project will be financially successful. If this is not the case, a careful examination of the resources will be required and whether any extraneous factors including the contract duration, the scope of service or the procurement route have increased the resource level.

Regardless, either the level of resource, contingency or profit will have to be adjusted to balance the fee. If the level of resource is reduced, the team leader may need to devise a strategy to ensure that the resource levels are not exceeded.

In conclusion, a resource plan that has been benchmarked against previous projects, has a contingency allocated for unforeseen events or aspects of re-design and is monitored, on a monthly basis, will result in a profitable project An ill-conceived plan, with no contingencies that is not monitored, is likely to result in a loss-making project.

9.6 Knowledge management

Increasingly, we are facing information overload as the internet, intranets, extranets, social media sites, and other digital communications within the project team allow fast and easy access to knowledge. At the same time, this information is not always so easily shared. It can end up sequestered in the hard drives or in the heads of project team members, where it is difficult to access and manage. To counter this, establishing a successful knowledge management system is essential to the success of a practice.

Architects channel information from many sources:

- precedent images from magazines or a practice's image library;
- plans of previous projects;
- statistics from previous projects, such as areas, construction values, form of procurement;
- latest research and thinking in subjects such as sustainability;
- new legislation including amendments to planning and building control legislation;
- British, or European, standards and, with more architects working internationally, international standards.

Knowledge management can be defined by asking: how can all these various strands of information be made readily available to each member of the project team, and how is it ensured that this information is current and up to date?

Successful strategies used by different companies to disseminate the correct knowledge include:

- Yellow Pages: a list of specialist subjects and people who have expertise in these subjects. This is likely to be of greater use in very large practices or organisations with several office locations;
- staff development: aligning strategies with staff training helps to imbed knowledge, and its location, into a practice's culture;
- web portals: utilising a practice intranet to facilitate fast access to key information via web portals;
- knowledge communities: encouraging specialists to communicate with each other.

Finally, the saying 'culture eats strategy for lunch' is pertinent here. You can provide all the knowledge needed to the fingertips of each member of staff but, until these staff culturally accept and use this information, your knowledge management system will not have worked.

9.7 Crisis management

Crisis management is a recent management trend that encourages businesses to consider what steps they might take if one of a number of scenarios were to arise. The logic is that, by rehearsing what would be done in a given scenario, any deficiencies within the practice can be identified and the business prepared for that eventuality. For example, what happens if there is a flood, a power cut or an IT systems failure?

Whether for temporary toilets or power supplies, contact names and arrangements can be sourced and then added to a single spreadsheet (frequently referred to as a continuity plan) that can be consulted if a particular crisis occurs. Good preparation and forward thinking can minimise the damage caused in the event of a crisis, bearing in mind that any damage can, among other things, have financial implications (in both the short and long term) or might even impact on the reputation of a company or affect staff morale.

Such principles are equally valid in the design management of a project and can be harnessed by a good team leader to assist with the design process. If risk management (as covered in Chapter 6) is the identification of risks and an analysis of the impact and probability of them occurring, then crisis management, from a design perspective, would be considering what alternative design solutions could be developed should a particular risk become problematic. In this regard, if a particular project risk has a number of solutions then, arguably, it is less of a risk (albeit a decision will be required by a given point in time to avoid delays to the design process), whereas a risk that has no alternative solution, or a solution with prohibitive costs, becomes a major project risk.

The point is that the lead designer and lead consultant can add value to the process by ensuring that their contributions to the project risk register make the **design** position clear in relation to each and every risk.

Conclusion to Chapter 9
Streamlining Practice Management

ONE — Continual improvements are essential if a practice is to maintain its competitive edge.

TWO — Benchmarking can provide statistical data which demonstrates that improvements are being made or to allow targets to be set for future improvements.

THREE — Post-occupancy evaluations might inform individual appraisals or be used to improve aspects of the way in which a practice works.

FOUR — If a team leader is to deliver a project successfully he/she must have the right resources available at the right time.

FIVE — If the project is not monitored carefully, it may make a loss, blighting the completion of an otherwise successful project.

SIX — Successful knowledge management ensures that the best possible knowledge is available to team members at all times.

SEVEN — Even the best planned project can encounter a crisis. Successfully dealing with a crisis demonstrates a leader's ability to react to unforeseen events quickly and efficiently.

CHAPTER 10
'SOFT SKILLS'

HAVING DISCUSSED the management tools applicable to the design process, in this chapter we consider the most important individual skills that a good lead consultant or lead designer and/or team leader must develop in order to manage the design process:

- *Communication* – effective communication is the core skill of a good leader. The increase in the variety of communication methods makes this task more difficult, but a good communicator will use the right means at the right time and achieve the right balance between meeting, phoning or e-mailing.
- *Delegation* – an effective leader needs to understand what to delegate and when. Successful delegation will allow him/her to consider strategic issues, plan for the future and deal calmly with issues before they become problematic and need to be resolved in a reactive manner.
- *Negotiation* – negotiation skills are required for numerous subjects: selling the design to the client, agreeing suitable fess or persuading a fellow designer to amend an aspect of the design.

By considering these skills and examining ways of improving core knowledge and understanding of them, a designer will become a better and more efficient leader.

10.1 Communication

Being a good communicator is one of the core competencies of effective team leaders, and this is particularly true for the lead consultant or lead designer, who needs to communicate with many and diverse parties on a wide-ranging set of subjects. The range of communication methods is huge – from e-mail to internal memos, and from letters to informal discussions – so, instead of looking at each individually, it is more instructive to learn from examples of poor communication, and how good managers might deal with these.

E-mail ping-pong

E-mailing back and forth will never resolve an issue. Indeed, the tone and meaning of e-mails can be interpreted in different ways by different people, making issues more difficult to resolve with each response. To overcome this, never e-mail a response to someone more than twice. It is best to discuss the issue over the phone, agree the way forward and then finalise the issue by responding with what was agreed during the call. If the matter is serious, organise an impromptu design workshop.

'It's your action!'

It might be correct to state to another party or individual that the 'the ball is in your court', but passing an unresolved action back to another party will not achieve resolution. As a team leader, you need to drive everything to conclusion, and that includes issues and actions that may lie with other parties.

Negative language

The morale and attitude of many people in the project team will be determined by the lead designer's language in a given situation, and a positive attitude can be backed up with positive language. In a design team meeting, if an issue is raised the means of resolving it should also be immediately stated. For example, 'We have an issue with the planners but we have sketched some options that we are presenting tomorrow' conveys an entirely different situation to the statement 'We have a problem with the planners'. There are always matters that need to be dealt with, but the way in which they are portrayed determines how your performance is perceived.

Hot topics

We have covered this subject elsewhere but it is essential to reiterate that, on any project, a number of key issues will exist at a given time. Effective communication is essential if such issues are to be driven to conclusion. Sometimes jumping on a train and meeting face to face with another designer, the client or a stakeholder is far more effective than trying to rely on electronic communication or a telephone call.

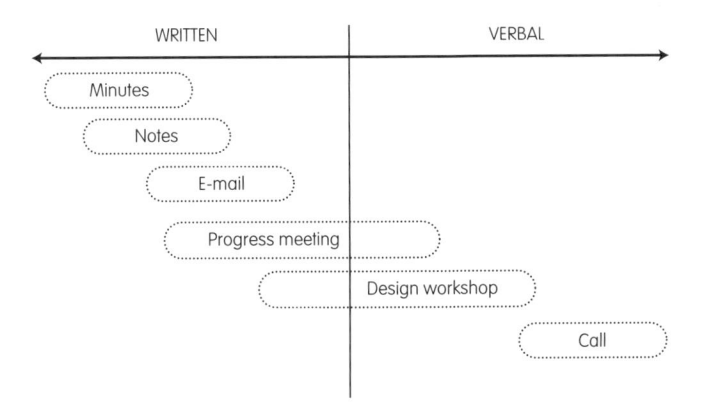

```
  WRITTEN              |              VERBAL
◄─────────────────────┼─────────────────────►
   (Minutes)           |
      (Notes)          |
        (E-mail)       |
         (Progress meeting)
              (Design workshop)
                       |    (Call)
```

FIGURE 10.1: Written versus verbal communication

Team bonding
Team events are becoming more customary, especially on larger projects where many people are involved. Individuals are more likely to cooperate with each other once they get to know one another and, as a team leader, you should not underestimate the benefits of such events.

'I owe you one'
Every designer on a project will have concerns that need to be resolved and many will require the co-operation and assistance of the lead designer. Refusing to listen to other designers will result in them not being co-operative when you have your own issues to resolve. However, this does not mean that you always have to give in to the demands of other designers, but it may be helpful to compromise occasionally so that when you encounter a situation that requires a particular effort from another designer, you can call in a favour in return.

Above all, effective communication is about determining the most appropriate means of communication for dealing with a given situation. Face-to-face meetings and telephone calls as well as e-mail are required, and Figure 10.1 illustrates how different means of project communication use different levels of written or verbal communication. Video conferencing and conference call technology can reduce the need for travel, although it needs to be remembered that face-to-face meetings (without the use of technology) are still beneficial on a regular basis.

10.2 Delegation

Delegation is one of the most important management skills.

Some people find it hard to begin to delegate work, mainly because they are delegating tasks they can do themselves and, when they first start to delegate to someone, they notice that the person is taking longer to complete the task than they would themselves. However, as responsibility increases, the need to delegate work to others becomes more and more essential, and failure to delegate will not leave time to plan the design work strategically.

To delegate a task effectively requires planning, briefing of the person undertaking the task, answering any queries they may have and ensuring that they are clear about timescales and the deliverables that are required. In this regard, delegation is a two-way process. Those delegating tasks must ensure that delegation happens properly. Just as significantly, those being delegated tasks must have the opportunity to ensure that they are briefed properly, are aware of what is required and when it is needed.

What points do I need to consider when delegating work?

When delegating work, consider the following:

- *Effective briefing* – is it clear exactly what the task is? Do team members understand exactly what deadlines they have to achieve and what is required for that deadline?
- *Reviewing* – time is required to monitor progress of tasks that have been delegated to ensure that they are progressing in line with your understanding. There is no point in waiting until the morning of a meeting to check whether someone has done exactly what was required.
- *Collaborative working* – team meetings are not only an effective method of establishing current priorities, the status of everyone's work and ensuring that no tasks are being duplicated or conflicting with one another. They are also an effective forum for delegating: delegating in a team environment can be more positively received, as staff will volunteer for tasks that they prefer as well as feeling more in control of their own destiny. Conversely, difficult or awkward tasks may not be taken up so a means of cajoling people to do these in such an environment needs to be considered.

- *Authority* – delegation of tasks is relatively straightforward; however, delegating authority is less so. Asking a team member to chair a design workshop requires confidence in the individual as the leader is relinquishing control of that activity. Practice-wide procedures, such as the use of a design status schedule, assist the delegation process as the means of running the workshop, and the output from it, is established. The output becomes a means of demonstrating that the workshop has been successfully run.
- *Delegate and manage* – remember that when tasks have been effectively delegated your time will be freed up to undertake design workshops on critical items, contact other designers to progress co-ordination items and to look at the programme to start planning future design activities. As noted above, time is also required for reviewing the progress of tasks that have been delegated or for reviewing the design work of other designers and subcontractors.
- *Incorrect information* – a good team leader will take responsibility for the whole team's performance. Placing the blame on a specific member of your team suggests that you were not adequately in control of your team or checking their output. If this occurs, absorb the criticisms, provide feedback to the team and discuss how the issue can be avoided in the future. If it is a major observation, provide feedback on practice-wide procedures.

10.3 Negotiation

Many architects and designers will not realise the extent to which they are effectively negotiating on a day-to-day basis. However, consider a number of everyday scenarios:

- requesting additional fees from the client;
- agreeing an amendment to an appointment document;
- requesting more resources at the weekly team leaders meeting;
- convincing the planners that a particular material is appropriate;
- persuading the M&E engineer that the plantroom strategy needs to be amended; or
- agreeing a different beam size with the C&S engineer to assist M&E co-ordination.

From this list it can be seen that a significant proportion of a designer's tasks requires good negotiation skills as well as the use of effective communication.

The following ten points will provide a better awareness of what is required to be a good negotiator – although remember that each point will not be relevant to every situation. As always with negotiation, be adaptable!

1. **Preparation** – rehearsing the reasoning for your decisions is essential but even more important is considering likely objections and why you believe that these are not relevant in the circumstances. A negotiation should not be narrowed down to just one issue. Discussing a number of items will make it less likely that the other party will realise which issue is most important to you.
2. **Questioning** – if you have made any assumptions or if any items in your reasoning are not clear, clarify these before you put your cards on the table. Assumptions need to be converted to facts before you commit to concluding negotiations on a specific point and to avoid discovering that the goalposts have moved in subsequent discussions.
3. **Listen** – listening to what the other party has to say on a specific point is essential. If several people disagree with your view then perhaps you need to reconsider before defending your position. The more retrenched you become, the harder it is to close the gap with another party. It is also essential to understand why the other party does not agree with your approach and you cannot constructively respond until you have fully listened to what they have to say.
4. **Winning every point** – you cannot win every argument so pick your battles well. A good negotiator will use this to their advantage, conceding issues that he/she does not feel strongly about, and refusing to budge on more crucial issues. Concede points slowly: giving in too easily tells the other party that you will probably be open to their views on other points. If possible, agree the points you want to have secured, before conceding on others. In that way, you will have secured your objectives and can take a harder line with the remaining ones.
5. **Negotiating position** – how strong is the position from which you are negotiating? For example, trying to agree additional fees after you have completed the work will be harder than agreeing them before you do the work. The 'I owe you one' tactic referred to above might need to be used to improve a position, but remember that such tactics cannot be used every time. At least create the appearance of strength. If the other party thinks you have no reason to compromise in your demands, he/she is less likely to ask you to.
6. **Attitude** – an abrasive or combative approach is more likely to lead to a breakdown in negotiations. Conversely, being co-operative and friendly or trying to take a collaborative stance is more likely to lead to a successful conclusion.

7. **Know when to stop** – in certain situations a stalemate will occur. If you cannot negotiate a position and have time to make a further presentation, take this opportunity. For example, 'we will get some samples and technical information and make a further presentation next week' might be an appropriate response. However, you also have to gauge, particularly where a client is involved, when a position cannot be improved.
8. **Be adaptable** – being able to adjust or adapt your strategies in response to the other parties' comments will gain a better outcome. Successful negotiators are those who can put forward viable alternatives while discussions are ongoing.
9. **The first offer** – often, the other party will make an offer they think you will refuse in order to establish their starting point. As such, it should never be accepted. You should respond with your initial offer, stating why you believe it is more appropriate. This then establishes the boundaries of the negotiation.
10. **The future** – in life, what goes around comes around. The goal in creating successful results is to have both parties feel that their objectives have been met, so that they will be willing to come back and work with each other again.

Conclusion to Chapter 10
'Soft Skills'

ONE — Effective communication is required to progress the design and many methods need to be used. A balance between formal (design team meeting) or informal (design workshops), face-to-face meetings, discussions on the phone or e-mail is required.

TWO — With more responsibility comes the need to delegate tasks. Delegating tasks allows you to accept more responsibility and to look ahead at forthcoming design matters.

THREE — Delegated tasks need to be monitored and reviewed to ensure that the desired result is achieved.

FOUR — A good negotiator has to have all the facts available in order to be successful, including an awareness of how far he/she is willing to move on a specific point.

INDEX

architectural designer 7, 10, 23

benchmarking 120-2, 123
briefing tracker 76-7
budget, design 61, 66
building integrated modelling (BIM) 35
building services *see* mechanical and electrical services (M&E)

change control 68-70, 75 (*see also* redesign)
checklists 94-5
civil and structural engineering (C&S) 10, 11, 21, 22-3, 24
client appointed design team 10, 12
client's brief 76-7 (*see also* employer's requirements)
collaborative working 33-6
communication 75, 129-31
concept stage 22-3, 43
construction cost plan 58, 59-67
construction programme 51-4
consultants 5-6 (*see also* design team; subconsultants)
   appointments 22, 34
   client-appointed team 12-13
   design reviews 101-4
   lead consultant appointed team 13-17
   novation 113
   use of term 13
continual improvement 75, 118-20
contract administrator role 7
contractor design 6, 27-33, 110 (*see also* design and build)
contractors (*see also* specialist subcontractors)
   early involvement 110
   post-tender negotiations 47-8
   programme 51-4
   tender price and contract sum 60
contractor's proposals 111

contractual structures 10-11, 112-16
co-ordinated design 20-1
co-ordination 19-26
   concept stage 22-3
   definitions 20
   design development stage 23-4
   production information stage 25
   reviews 103-4
   technical design stage 24-5
cost consultant 10, 11, 17, 57, 58
cost estimating 62-4
cost management 57-72
   change control 68-70
   consultant roles 57-9
   cost estimating 62-4
   cost plan 58, 59-60, 65-6
   design budget 61, 66
   value management 71
   whole life costs 66-7
cost per square metre 62, 63
cost plan 58, 59-67
crisis management 126
critical path 53-4

delegation 132-3
descriptive specification clause 30
design and build 28, 111, 113-14
design budget 61, 66
design checklists 94-5
design dependency 49-51
design development stage 23-4, 45
design intent drawings 31-2
design management, definition 3-4
design quality indicator 120
design responsibility matrix 83-5
design reviews 25, 97, 98-9, 101-7
design status schedule 21-2, 44, 66, 86-91

design team (see also consultants)
   appointments 22
   client-appointed 10, 12–13
   collaborative working 33–6
   contractual structures 10–11
   co-ordination 19–26
   design responsibility matrix 83–5
   integrated working 16, 26–33
   lead consultant appointed 10–11, 12–13
   meetings 78
   performance monitoring 17
   progress reports 80–2
   structure 10–18
design workshops 24, 26, 66, 79

employer's agent role 7
employer's requirements 77, 111 (see also client's brief)

facilities management 67
fee proposal 15
financial risks 16
fire strategy 92–3

general arrangement (GA) drawings 21, 22–3, 24, 43

health and safety 88
historical data 59, 62, 63

integrated working 16
integration, design 26–33
iterative design 41–8

knowledge management 125–6

lead consultant
   cost management role 57, 58–9
   duties 5–9, 37–8
   management roles 6–9

lead designer
   cost management role 58
   design reviews 25, 101–2
   design team appointment 10–11
   duties 5–9, 38–9
   management roles 6–9
leadership roles 2, 6
lead-in period 47

maintenance strategy 67, 93
management contracting 33, 115
management reviews 100
management roles 6–9
master programme 40–1
mechanical and electrical services (M&E) 10, 11, 21, 23, 24, 63–4
meetings 78 (see also workshops)
monitoring payments 16
monitoring progress 52–3, 82

negotiation 122–5
novation 113

package design 33, 115
performance indicators 120
performance monitoring 17, 120–2
performance specified work 27, 29–30
planned vs actual progress 52–3
post-occupancy evaluation 122–3
prescriptive specification clause 30
pre-tender estimate 47, 60
private finance initiative (PFI) 67, 115–16
procurement 109–16
   design and build 113–14
   management contracting 115
   private finance initiative (PFI) 115–16
   traditional 112
production information stage 25, 46–8, 101

INDEX

programme compression 40–1
programme float 54
programming design 37–55 (*see also* work stage programmes)
   concept stage 43
   construction programme 51–4
   design dependency 49–51
   design development stage 45
   design status schedule 44
   iterative design 41–4
   master programme 40–1
   production information stage 46–8
   technical design stage 46
progress meetings 78
progress monitoring 52–3, 82
progress reports 44–5, 80–2
project brief 76–7
project management, definition 3
project manager role 7
project meetings 78 (*see also* design workshops)
project quality plan 35, 74–5
project statistics 121–2
prototyping 42

quality plan 35, 74–5, 118

redesign 41, 61, 63 (*see also* change control)
reports, progress 44–5, 80–2
resource management 123–4
reviews 97–108
   consultants information 101–3
   design reviews 25, 97, 98–9, 101–7
   management reviews 100
   specialist subcontractors 104–7
RIBA work stages *see* work stage programmes
risk management 12–17, 89–91, 110–11

'shop drawings' 27
software compatibility 35
specialist consultants 5–6
specialist subcontractors 28
   design dependency 31, 48–9
   design reviews 105–7
   package design 33
strategies 67, 92–3
subconsultants 10
   appointment 15, 34
   integrated working 16
   monitoring payments 16
   performance monitoring 17
   reviews 104
   selection 14–15, 34
   use of term 13

technical design stage 24–5, 46
terms of appointment 6, 22, 34
third party organisations 40
3D drafting 35
trade contractor 28
traditional procurement 112

uncertainty 43–4

value engineering 71
value management 71

whole life costs 66–7
work packages 33, 115
work stage programmes 37–9
   content 43, 45–8
   co-ordination at each RIBA stage 22–5
   dealing with uncertainty 43–4
   overlapping 40–1
   reconciliation 39
works contractor 28
workshops 24, 26, 66, 79, 89–91

139